The Power of Dance:
Partner Dance From Ballroom to Olympic Sport

Setsuko Tsuchiya, PhD

Savant Books and Publications
Honolulu, HI, USA
2022

Savant Books and Publications LLC
1545 Ala Mahamoe St.
Honolulu, HI 96819 USA
http://www.savantbooksandpublications.com

Printed in the USA

Edited by Chizuru "Lucy" Takeda
Cover image "Seamless Dance Steps" #468111154 by dikobraziy (with permission iStock by Getty Images).
Cover by Daniel S. Janik

Copyright 2021 by Setsuko Tsuchiya. All rights reserved. No part of this work may be reproduced without the prior written permission of the author.

13 digit ISBN: 978-1-7376431-6-6

This book is primarily non-fictional; though the information conveyed comes from different sources, every effort has been made to make this work as accurate as possible. However, there may remain mistakes, both typographical and in content. Information conveyed is current up to the printing date.

The author and publisher have neither liability nor responsibility to any person or entity with respect to any loss or damage caused, or alleged to have been caused, directly or indirectly, by the information conveyed in this book.

Daniel S. Janik and Albert Franz have kindly reviewed this work.

First Edition: September 2022
Library of Congress Control Number: 2022947049

Dedication

I dedicate this book to my dance partner and mentor, Daniel S. Janik, who encouraged me to keep at it and never give up.

Acknowledgements

Thank you to Chizuru "Lucy" Takeda, who has been far more than an editor; rather, a staunch supporter of this work and my right hand. Special thanks to Mr. Albert Franz, my dance instructor and coach for over 20 years, whose style remains unique in the world of DanceSport. My special thanks to Mr. and Ms. Yuki, special dance advisors who are busily imparting their own take on partnered competitive ballroom dancing to me. Additional thanks to Ms. Anne Ho and her dance partner Glen Okazaki for encouraging me to always dance at the highest level possible. Thanks to Mr. Geoffrey Fells for teaching me all about competition, and Aya Terazawa, my friend and companion throughout the years we worked together under at the Hawaii Star Ball. Additional thanks to Mr. Roger Izumigawa, former Commissioner of DanceSport for the Pacific Region. Finally, heartfelt thanks to Yoshiko Fujioka, Mr. and Mrs. Tsukioka and Mr. and Mrs. Tamamori, all longtime personal friends with whom my partner and I have had the pleasure of dancing over the years.

Table of Contents

Foreword by Albert Franz — 1

Chapter 1 - **History and Definitions** — 5

Chapter 2 - **American Style Smooth and Rhythm Dance** — 29

Chapter 3 - **International-Style Ballroom Dance** — 45

Chapter 4 - **International-Style Latin-American Dance** — 69

Chapter 5 - **DanceSport** — 103

Chapter 6 - **DanceSport, Partnership and Power Exchange** — 111

Chapter 7 - **Olympic DanceSport** — 123

Chapter 8 - **Gender, Sexual Orientation, Race, Culture and Age** — 133

Chapter 9 - **Partnered Ballroom Dance** — 173

Chapter 10 - **The Future** — 187

About the Author — 212

Thesis: Partner dancing is at the heart of the power of dance. This work is taken, in part, from my doctoral dissertation, "The Power of Partnered Ballroom Dance " in fulfillment of a PhD in Performing Arts in Ballroom and Latin Dance Performance.

Foreword

When I first read this work you are holding in your hands, Dr. Setsuko Tsuchiya's book, THE POWER OF DANCE, it took me down Memory Lane for sure, bringing to mind many of the people who were influential in ballroom dance, and my own dance career. Those mentioned were well known in their days as pioneering teachers, dancers and authors, coaches, many being world class champion competitors as well.

In America, it was Fred Astaire, in my opinion, who was far superior a partner ballroom dancer compared to the many other social dance gurus of the time. Yet, it was the "Author Murray Dance Hour," the TV show back in the 50s, which became the forerunner for today's "Dancing with the Stars." During that time there was also the Lawrence Welk Show that everyone was watching on Saturday night, and the Mickey Mouse Club on daily for kids. Setsuko mentions Dick Clark's "American Bandstand" broadcast from Philadelphia.

Interestingly, the dance pioneers mentioned were probably better known in England than in the USA. Here, it was the music that was well known, and everyone just wanted to dance to the lively music. I still remember Perez Prado in the movie Underwater, where he introduced "Cherry Pink and Apple Blossom White" which became the first Cha Cha Cha.

Most of the people mentioned in this wonderful book, I have personally known or at least known of, having been coached, examined or judged by many. As an up-and-coming competitor and professional dance teacher, it was essential that we get "qualified" and back then that meant reaching Membership level in the Imperial Society of Teachers of Dancing, OF LONDON, not USA!

After passing the Associate exam and teaching for two years, one could then take the Membership exam. Once a member, one could finally categorically state that he or she was a qualified dance instructor and judge of Ballroom or Latin-American dance. Taking the exam was very stressful because the English have always seen themselves superior to us Americans.

It is astonishing to me that Dr. Tsuchiya's book included so many pioneering personalities that I knew and respected. For example, back then, Mr. Dimitri Petrides, a very talented Latin Dancer, had a wife, Nina Hunt, who became the "Teacher to the Champions." The Japanese Champions all trained in Latin with Nina Hunt!

I recall Doris Lavelle, who with her partner, Monsieur Pierre, went from England to Cuba to acquire "the Rumba technique." She then wrote THE book on "Latin Technique." I recall her original book having photos of her Cuban teacher on the veranda overlooking the sea. I studied for my exams from that book with the help of Elizabeth Romain, Alex Moore's "girl Friday."

As for the future of Olympic DanceSport, incredibly, so far only break dancing has become an actual Olympic event. Still, I do hope that Setsuko's prediction of something like World DanceSport becoming World Olympic DanceSport will come true. The big question, in my mind, is whether it will even be recognizable as having originated from partnered ballroom dance. We shall have to see.

I vividly remember reading a sign in a Virginia ice rink: "If you have any idea of your child being in the Olympics, be prepared to spend about $22,000 a year." That was in 1980-81, so you can imagine the cost today whether it be ice or ballroom dancing. The ice rink was broken into "patches," each had to be rented separately for practice. In addition, each competitor needed 1) boots, 2) blades, 3) coaching, 4) towels and 5) costumes, collectively very expensive. I mention this because I was deeply involved in teaching ice dancing to ice skaters from 1977-80. Believe me, those kids were athletes, and some actually went on to the Olympics, starting with the Lake Placid Winter Olympics.

I recall how subjective the judging was for these events back then: not like baseball with a winning team, or track in which the winner was the first to break the ribbon.

It's my personal observation that dancing is, as Setsuko states, one of the best exercises for well being. THE POWER OF DANCE really brings this to mind. Some Japanese have apparently known this "secret" all along. I remember that when I went to Tokyo in 1977, the World Professional Ballroom and Latin Dance Championships, Japan had 400 professional competitors. There might be maybe only 50 Americans in a similar American competition. When I went to Tokyo in 1977 for the World Professional Championships in Ballroom and Latin Dance, we entered the BUDOKAN and saw 10,000 spectators. We Americans (two couples in each division, the Champion and #2) were flabbergasted. Never had we had in the USA such a turnout in spectators. It was after that trip to Tokyo that, on return to the USA, the package tour stopped in Honolulu for three days and I fell in love with Hawaii. I met Setsuko Tsuchiya and her partner, Daniel S. Janik when I re located from my home in Washington D.C.

    I hope you will enjoy this incredible book as much as you can see I have.

- Albert Franz (2022)

Chapter 1
History and Definitions

Young or old, everyone dances:
   Infants and children delight in expressing themselves at almost any opportunity by moving to music. Teens, nervous about the idea of being held closely, will nonetheless dance with a new partner with reckless abandon at gatherings, parties and other social events. Adults also find considerable enjoyment in pairing with a partner and moving gracefully together as one. Dancing is always around and with us, providing pleasure, enjoyment, relaxation and exercise. It seems natural that something as universal as dance would not only be practiced, but studied and perfected. Not just as an art or science, but as a universal philosophical ideal. (Tsuchiya)
   As a young child, I danced alongside my parents at the annual Bon Dance festivals in Japan. As a preteen, I savored with my friends the joy of Japanese social folk dancing. As a young adult, I began evening ballroom dance lessons at City Hall, where I learned basic Waltz, Tango, Rumba, Cha Cha Cha and Jitterbug, much to my parents' chagrin. Later, when I

moved to California, I met my future husband and lifelong dance partner at a YMCA dance.

We eventually moved to Hawaii, and there we enjoyed taking American-style Ballroom and Rhythm dance lessons from a former Arthur Murray instructor, Ms. Judy Athans. Later, as keen amateurs, we started International-style performance and competition partner ballroom dance lessons with Mr. Albert Franz, seven times North American Ten Dance Champion and International DanceSport Adjudicator. More recently my husband and I have begun working with professional Japanese International-style Ballroom and Latin-American dance coaches Seiji and Hiromi Yuki, focusing on health and the use of body, individual muscles and nerves in dance. During this time, we've had the pleasure of working with Mr. Glenn Okazaki and Ms. Anne Ho, USA Senior Amateur Ballroom Finalists, as well as taking brief lessons from such notables as Tony Meredith and Melanie LaPatin (1996); Alain Doucet/Anik Jolicoeur (1997); Ms. Leialoha (1997); Mr. Geoffrey Fells (1997); Tomasz and Izabela Lewandowski (2005); Ms. Heather Smith (2005); Christopher Hawkins and Justyna Kozinska (2006); Urs Geisenhainer (2006); Igor and Irina Suvorov (2006); Yoshihiro and Tomoko Miwa (2014); Mr. Carlos Chang (2017); Mariusz Zakrzewski and Lynnsay Ray Robertson (2018); Ms. Eriko Shimazaki (2018); Mr. Koichiro Tsukioka (2019); and Mr. Marco Camarlinghi (2019).

Any discussion of ballroom dancing should be prefaced with some basic definitions. For this work, I would like to define "ballroom dancing" as *partnered* Ballroom/Smooth/Standard and/or Rhythm/Latin-American dancing by at least one couple on a ballroom floor. Unfortunately, the term "ballroom" has been used to mean both (1) Smooth/Standard/Ballroom and Rhythm/Latin-American dances danced on a ballroom floor, AND (2) collectively just the Smooth/Standard/Ballroom dances danced on a ballroom floor. This can cause considerable confusion. *In this work, "ballroom dancing" includes both partnered Smooth/Standard/Ballroom dances AND Rhythm/Latin-American dances unless otherwise stated.* While most would agree that ballroom dancing requires a partner, one can practice and take lessons without a partner. Nor does one have to have one particular partner for all ballroom dances. Still, the inclusion of the word "partnered" in the above definition is of great importance when considering the power of dance.

Ballroom dancing can be social, keen amateur, performance or competitive in nature. Most ballroom dancing will be in the American-style (Smooth and/or Rhythm) or International-style (Ballroom/Standard and/or Latin-American); however, social dance can include any mix of "styles," e.g. a social dance might include Nightclub Two-Step. Nowadays, DanceSport, an evolving form of ballroom dance, has begun challenging the boundaries and limits of both the American and International styles, creating a "new" style of its own.

Ironically, USA Dance (formerly the United States Amateur Ballroom Dancers Association and current certifying body of DanceSport Athlete competitors within the USA) offers no formal definition other than at the "competitive" level. It is couples dancing Waltz, Foxtrot, Tango, Viennese Waltz, and Bolero, Rumba, Cha Cha, Mambo and East Coast Swing in the American Style, and/or Waltz, Quickstep, Foxtrot, Tango, Viennese Waltz, and Rumba, Cha Cha Cha, Samba, Jive and Paso Doble in the International style ("Competitor Guide").

A more detailed definition might be "Ballroom dancing is a *partnership* dance where couples, using step-patterns, move rhythmically, expressing the characteristics of music...Foxtrot, Waltz, Tango, Viennese Waltz and Quickstep...East Coast Swing, Jive, Rumba, Bolero, Cha Cha, Mambo, Samba and Paso Doble. Popular dances, such as the Argentine Tango, Salsa, Merengue, West Coast Swing, Hustle, Bachata, Night Club 2-Step and County and Western Dancing, are more recent additions to the world of Ballroom dance" ("What is Ballroom Dancing?"— the italics are mine).

Although Wikipedia is not a generally favored academic source, based solely on the number of adherents, ballroom dancing is primarily a social rather than a performance/competitive activity. Wikipedia being a social media website, offers a more comprehensive definition of ballroom dance. "Ballroom dance may refer, at its widest definition, to almost any recreational dance *with a partner*...The term 'ballroom dancing' is derived from the word ball which in turn originates from the Latin word ballet which means 'to dance' (a ballroom being a large room specially designed for such dances)" ("Ballroom dance"). To this I would add, usually by a number of couples on a ballroom floor.

According to Picart, DanceSport is "When this self-expressive, free-flowing dance takes on a stricter format, follows a syllabus and specific steps and moves are judged by an international criteria, ballroom dancing becomes dance sport."

On the other hand, DanceSport, according to the World DanceSport Federation or WDSF, "has become an all-encompassing brand for an activity that is uniquely accessible and sociable, allowing participants to improve physical fitness and mental well-being, to interact, and to obtain results at all levels. Everybody is capable of moving to music. And dance transgresses all barriers of age, gender and culture" (World DanceSport Federation "About DanceSport").

In fact, DanceSport, which seems to have evolved as a segue from ballroom dancing to Olympic DanceSport, has yet to be officially recognized by the International Olympic Committee. However, in 1995, the International DanceSport Federation or IDSF, the precursor to WDSF, "was officially recognized by the International Olympic Committee (IOC) as the representative body for DanceSport...to be included in the Olympic Program...[An] essential part of the IDSF's mission was campaigning to bring DanceSport to the Olympics" (Pyles). Therefore, at present, one can assume that

IDSF's definition of DanceSport might be a particularly good one. That is, "DanceSport is the activity that *combines sport and dance*, and that allows the participants to improve physical fitness and mental well-being, to form social relationships and to obtain results in competition at all levels. Competitive DanceSport in a wide variety of dance styles and forms *is practised within the internationally recognised and organised competition structure of IDSF*" (World DanceSport Federation "DanceSport for All!"; the italics are mine).

USA Dance, the U.S. National Member body of the WDSF, on the other hand, defines DanceSport as "competitive ballroom dancing...basically *couples* assembled on a dance floor being compared with other couples by qualified judges, on relative performance and execution using a defined and recognized set of standards. USA Dance competitors are called DanceSport Athletes" (USA Dance "What is DanceSport?"; again, the italics are mine).

Historically, "Dance turned into genuine sport at the beginning of the twentieth century, when French entrepreneur Camille de Rhynal and a group of superb dancers added the competitive to the social, and when they converted ballrooms into the venue for their contests" (World DanceSport Federation "About DanceSport").

WDSF, while attempting to be all-encompassing in reference to DanceSport, unfortunately doesn't strictly define it. This, in my opinion, is a good example of why the relationship between DanceSport and the Olympics remains obscure.

So obscure that recently, USA Dance admitted Breakdance, essentially *un-partnered* street dancing, into its fold. NOTE: Breakdancing is now an official Olympic sport scheduled for 2024 Paris games; DanceSport is not (World DanceSport Federation. "Breaking officially added to Olympic Games Paris 2024").

Picart mentioned that IDSF president Hegemann "visibly skewed" framing of the problem in that IDSF was interested in the *sport*, while the World Dance and Dance Sport Council (WD&DSC), at the time, the world authority for Professional Dancing, was simply focused on its "livelihood and personal future."

On the other hand, sport, in general, "is defined by international organisations such as the United Nations or the Council of Europe for the purpose of establishing their sports-related policies. 'Sport means all forms of physical activity which, through casual or organised participation, aim at improving physical fitness and mental well-being, forming social relationships or obtaining results in competition at all levels.' European Sports Charter. WDSF adheres to the wording and defines DanceSport accordingly" (World DanceSport Federation "DanceSport for All!").

In other words, DanceSport is in a state of flux, albeit to be better positioned for admission into the Olympics:

> In recent years, the IOC began worrying the Olympics were seen as boring, stuffy and irrelevant, particularly to young people...So the IOC be-

gan looking to make the Games more youth-oriented, trading the classic events for things 21st-century youngsters actually do in their spare time. It had been successful in steering towards youth in the winter Olympic world, when snowboarding was added to the 1998 Nagano Games. 'We want to take sport to the youth'...After inviting submissions from sporting federations around the world, surfing, rock climbing, skateboarding and three-on-three basketball were chosen to be included on the 2020 Olympics schedule in Tokyo. (Keoghan)

DanceSport, however, is not generally considered a "youth" sport that "youngsters actually do in their spare time."

According to Picart, IDSF and IOC, had, from the start, conflicting views about DanceSport as an Olympic event. Eventually, in 1996, IDSF received a thousand dollar "welcome gift" from the IOC. The general agreement that resulted unified amateurs and professionals into a single competitive group. Later, in a bid to become the sole recognized representative of Olympic DanceSport, WD&DSC and IDSF got into conflict with each other. IDSF proclaimed it had signed International Management Group (IMG), the world-renowned sport management group, to develop DanceSport for the Olympics. In 1997, IDSF, now the WDSF received "full" IOC recognition.

IDSF, again according to Picart, wrote competition regulations, strongly emphasizing the "sport" image of DanceSport over dance as a performing art in order to move DanceSport closer to Olympic recognition.

DanceSport, however, still lacked one major criteria to become an Olympic sport: namely, it needed to have a recognizable medal status in order to be presented alongside other medalist sports.

The American Tradition

I would like to begin this book from the American Tradition, being as I began seriously studying ballroom dancing after I came to the USA, and in may aspects, ballroom dance as we know it today began in the Americas.

Dance is assumed to have first emerged when people began moving together, first individually and in groups, later as partners. It is from this common perspective that Stephenson and Iaccarino mentioned, "There is no ancient civilization of which we have record that did not know dancing...[and] no nation held dancing in higher esteem or cultivated it for aesthetic values more than the ancient Greeks."

Partnered ballroom dancing as we know it today is a recent phenomenon initiated within, and to some extent, remaining a part of "high" society. Ballroom dancing, whether social, keen amateur, but especially performance and competition, was and remains an expensive, elitist affair.

Stephenson and Iaccarino held that, "people dance for one reason only: enjoyment," claiming that partnered "social dance is one of the most important male-female interactions in our society," teaching "poise, manners, and how to relate comfortably to the opposite sex in a time when sexual freedom is placing increased pressures on our young people." In addition, ballroom dancing is "good exercise, good fun, and something you can do all your life." With ballroom dancing, there is said to be no "generation gap," though recently, mid to post COVID, USA Dance has added non-partnered "break dancing" into its fold, implying both a definite generation gap and the inclusion of non-partnered "pop" or "hip-hop" dance with only youthful athletes participating (How break dancing).

To social dance, I would add—excluding contemporary break dancing—"dancing in *partnership*...in performance and competition" (Tsuchiya).

It is often said that the earliest partnered social dances were European folk and peasant couple dances like the Basse and Pavanes—formal, stately dances done with gliding steps. In or around the sixteenth century, Contredanse and the Minuet led to the formal cotillion. In the 1700s Quadrilles and Lancers appeared at cotillions (Stephenson & Iaccarino).

It is generally held that there was little to no ballroom-style dancing in the Native American Western hemisphere outside of Spanish Mexico. However, a distinction between performers and spectators had already long existed in Native

American dance. After a performance, the dancers often joined in one or another less-formal social dances designed to unite participants and observers in partnership dance. Additionally, the leader and helper were typically of opposite moiety (Native American cultures typically allowed intersex individuals). When women entered a dance, singly or with another, they typically paired with a different moiety. Finally, Native Americans often danced on geometric ground plans analogous to contemporary ballroom floors, circling counter-sunwise (counterclockwise or widdershins) (Kurath).

While dancing is the main focus of this book, one must always acknowledge the music behind the dances; Stephenson and Iaccarino appropriately referenced "the first American-printed music book" published in 1556 in Mexico City.

Around 1686, the first professional social dance masters began advertising to "socialites" and "social climbers' in newspapers in both London and New York City. Even so, it was different for "working people." On the lower end of the social stratum, bars and brothels provided the majority of entertainment. For the upwardly mobile lower class in smaller cities and towns, the public dance hall provided community activities such as town meetings, talks by visiting speakers and dances. In larger cities, the dance halls were strictly commercial and served liquor, often attracting a rougher crowd. In such places, public dance halls served as a meeting place for boys and men to meet girls and women, sometimes to the point of providing sexual opportunities. Considered particularly socially distasteful were the "dime-a-dance," or Taxi-dance halls which remained active through World War II (Stephenson & Iaccarino).

The New York dance masters generally stated purpose at this time was to "teach manners" to the socially mobile. Ward McAllister, a professional New York dance master, for example, was offering dance classes for "social elevation." According to Stephenson and Iaccarino, McAllister offered ongoing "by invitation only" family circle dance classes. For high society, dancing the latest dances was considered a required skill.

After immigrating to the USA, English-born composer and soon to become rogue New York dance master, Allen T. Dodworth opened his famous New York dance academy (The Pasadena Star-News). Interestingly, in Dodworth's 1885 book *Dancing and its Relation to Education and Social Life: With a New Method of Instruction*, he emphatically stated that dancing was not just for social amusement; rather, it dealt with "matters to do with men's souls."

During this time, churches expressed mixed feelings about dancing, sometimes encouraging and other times discouraging it. The Catholic Church, the dominant religion, was said to generally regard dancing as a useful "safety valve" for youth (Stephenson & Iaccarino).

Ballroom dancing as we know it today, is said by Stephenson & Iaccarino as well as Reynolds to have started with the Viennese Waltz. This fast waltz, begun as an "open-hold,"Austrian, peasant dance—notably the Nachantz or Volta—was popularized in high society by modification to include the "closed hold" and later "close, closed hold."

If ballroom dance in America at this time was still largely in the European (later International) style, then Latin-American dance was distinctly more American in the sense that four of the five Latin American dances came from Cuba (Rumba and Cha Cha Cha), Brazil (Samba) and USA (Jive). Paso Doble, on the other hand, came to America from Europe via France though it originated in Spain (Tsuchiya).

Once in America, most of the European ballroom dances as well as the Latin-American dances, which for purposes of this work are included in the general term "ballroom dances," quickly took on a distinctly American styling.

The Viennese or "Fast" Waltz, or simply Waltz, was initially met with skepticism and recrimination. "Dancing masters at once saw the waltz as a threat to their profession. The minuet and other court dances required considerable practice, not only to learn the many complex figures, but also to develop suitable postures and deportment. The basic steps of the waltz could be learned in relatively short time, often just by observation." It was also criticized on moral grounds by those opposed to the close hold (Stephenson & Iaccarino).

In the United States, the Waltz was said to have been first danced in Boston in 1834 by Lorenzo Papanti who demonstrated it in Mrs. Otis' Beacon Hill mansion (Stephenson & Iaccarino). By this time, it had changed from the rather fast

Valse à deux temps ("waltz in two beats"), to the slower, more danceable Valse à deux pas ("waltz of two steps"), and, with the addition of the one, three, four, five and seven step variations, became popularized as "The Boston." [Clarke & Crisp; Boston (dance)]. The Boston almost entirely disappeared during World War I, but is said by Stephenson and Iaccarino to have stimulated the revival and development of the English or International-style Slow Waltz.

By 1840, the Waltz was accompanied by a second, partnered, closed-hold dance, the Polka. By the early 1900s, traditional ballroom dances like the Quadrilles, Lancers and other open, couple dances were already being replaced by the English Two-Step, One Step, Foxtrot and Tango (Stephenson & Iaccarino).

Historically, Stephenson and Iaccarino attribute Spanish, Indian, Portuguese, African and French (creole) cultural influences as providing the foundations of American ballroom dance. In the United States of America, where some eight million Africans of color had been imported as slaves, a new rhythm and accent appeared, not on the downbeat as in Europe, but on the up- or off-beat, introducing syncopation as evidenced by Scott Joplin's popular ragtime music (Reynolds).

In *The History of Dance*, Mary Clarke and Clement Crisp further describe the Cakewalk, a high-stepping African-American vaudeville dance popular in the late 1800s, replete with stylized costumes: a tall black hat, tall white collar, black coat and tails for men, and elaborate swirling frocks for women, that, brilliantly performed, acquired an increasingly theatrical flavor and popularity as it progressed through the southern states to New York.

The 1900's brought rapid city growth, attracting vast numbers of immigrants and young people into the cities. With limited money and no radio, television, movies, cars, cell phones or computers, young "good" men and women discovered public dance halls instead of bars and brothels. Social dance halls had served in smaller cities as centers for community activities. In larger cities, they sadly remained almost strictly commercial.

The Cakewalk, which quickly became popular on the vaudeville circuit, was a precursor to the single most popular ballroom dance of all time, the Foxtrot. Stephenson and Iaccarino claimed that the Foxtrot by name, was first danced in the Garden de Dance on the roof of the New York Theater. In 1914, as part of an act downstairs, Harry Fox was doing trotting steps to ragtime music which people called "Fox's Trot." Wishing to capitalize on this, management introduced the dance with Cakewalk elegance upstairs and modern ballroom dancing began in earnest.

From roughly 1890 to 1920, the "Two-Step," one of many variations of The Boston, rose to popularity. Technically a Valse à deux temps danced to 4/4 or 3/4 time and waltz tempo, it rose to fame with the appearance of John Philip Sousa's "march-like" music, declining with the onset of the Jazz era.

The "English Two Step" in particular provided a segue to the ever popular American and International Foxtrot (Stephenson & Iaccarino; Albert Franz, personal communique). In fact, when I first studied International style Slow Foxtrot, my coach, USA Ten Dance Champion and International DanceSport Adjudicator Mr. Albert Franz began by teaching me the "English Two Step" later adding progression, transforming it into Slow Foxtrot.

At the end of the 1800s, everyone was dancing the Polka, Schottische, Two-Step, and Waltz. According to Stephenson & Iaccarino, twentieth century dancing entirely changed due to the introduction of ragtime music. Everything, of course, except Waltz.

Ragtime is a form of music usually in 2/4 or "cut" time. Ragtime was all about syncopation. The word Ragtime came from people asking music stores for "ragged" music (Stephenson & Iaccarino).

In *The Complete Book of Ballroom Dancing*, Stephenson and Iaccarino stated that Tango originated in Spain. Andalusian, or Spanish Tango was initially danced solo by a woman. I was impressed with a performance of the "Flamenco Tangos" (a *palos* or school of Flamenco related roughly to the Rumba Flamenca) by Romani dancers during a visit to Spain in 2003. I was actually looking into the history and music of Paso Doble at the time, but found myself wondering if Argentine, American and International Tango might be related to Flamenco Tangos given their strong, highly stylized, abrupt movements.

Stephenson and Iaccarino stated that with time, Andalusian Tango became danced by one or two couples walking together, typically playing castanets. In the nineteenth century, the Tango Argentino became popular with the lower classes of Buenos Ares particularly in the Barrio de las Ranas. From there, it spread throughout the world.

In 1903, at fourteen years of age, Maurice Mouvet, a Belgian born in New York City, moved with his family to Paris, where he began dancing in the cafés of Paris. His interest in Tango supposedly peaked during a visit to the Café de Paris, where he witnessed a party of South Americans dancing "Argentine Tango." He returned to New York City with his dance partner, Florence Walton, where together they introduced their version of the Tango alongside the Apache (L'Apache) or "Bowery Waltz" (Stephenson & Iaccarino; Bowery Waltz).

Vernon and Irene Castle

Social dance was given a tremendous boost just before World War I by Vernon and Irene Castle. Born in England, William Vernon Blyth came to New York in 1906 and began appearing on the vaudeville stage as a comic actor, magician, singer and dancer. He married vaudeville actress Irene Foote and the two went to Paris to take part in a musical show, "The Hen-Pecks." The show lasted only a short time, and they turned, out of desperation, to exhibition dancing in cafés and restaurants. Befriended by "Papa Louis," owner of the Café de Paris, they began giving nightly performance-exhibitions using the stage names Vernon and Irene Castle. After an outstanding year in Paris, they returned to America. Adopted by New York City society, they established Castle House as a studio for lessons in "refined" ballroom dancing to live music played by the Castle House Orchestra. In their book, *Modern Dancing*, they described the One-Step or Castle Walk, Hesitation Waltz, Tango Argentine and Tango Bresilienne or Maxixe. They emphasized grace, beauty, natural walking movement and classical (meaning slower tempo) dances (Castle).

Irene Castle distinguished between "afternoon tea" (social) dancing and "evening formal" or keen amateur ballroom dancing, in the process not only establishing a uniquely "American" dancing style, but also influencing dress. For example, she endorsed the elastic Castle Corset, recommending pleated petticoats with lace to hide the ankles, silk stockings with at most two pairs of garters, silk bloomers and a new French undergarment called a "brassiere." She was the first to popularize looseness in the sleeves to prevent binding when the arms were raised. Comfortable shoes, such as pumps, with a moderate heel held firmly in place with ribbons, completed a dance costume that would be not unfamiliar to ballroom dancers today. Ballroom dancing as envisioned by Vernon and Irene was exclusive and expensive. It soon became both a pastime and a signature of the wealthy and socially privileged. The Castles began a new era in

American partner dance, namely that of American-franchised dance studios. Over the years, these studios trained millions of dancers each in their own unique styles and figures.

Vernon and Irene Castle established Castle Park at Coney Island "so that vacationing New Yorkers could keep up with their dance lessons." Soon the exclusive Castle Club and Castles-by-the-Sea were established. In 1914, the Castles appeared together in a musical named "Watch Your Step" with songs written especially for them by Irving Berlin. By 1915, they were performing regularly at Castles-in-the-Air, a rooftop-garden above the Forty-Fourth Street Theater, at the outrageous salary of $1,500 a week—American ballroom dancing had come of age.

At the same time, from 1913 to 1914, the Tango Argentine craze peaked, causing dance halls to assume an increasingly "bad name" especially in the "tango district" of New York (Stephenson & Iaccarino).

Interestingly, after World War I, Tango's habanera music—the dance of Havana, with its four-beat unit that skips the second pulse, instead sounding on the second half of the beat, its slower tempo and longer steps—changed to milonga, with its syncopated eight beats accenting the first (sometimes also second), fourth, fifth, and seventh beats. Its faster tempo and shorter, quicker, more abrupt steps made it increasingly popular (Stephenson & Iaccarino; Deasy).

At about the same time as the Castles, a musical show called "Over the River," originating in San Francisco, played in New York, featuring a new dance called the "Turkey Trot." During the performance, dancers were called to move like various animals or scenes, eventually resulting in the Grizzly Bear, Bunny Hug, Boston Dip, Shiver Dance, Lover' Two-step, Hug-Me-Close, and Gaby Glide. One-step figures, imminently popular because of their inherent ease and one-step-per-beat rhythm, at the same time began changing into what would be recognized today as the Foxtrot and American Peabody (Stephenson & Iaccarino).

Arthur Murray

Arthur Murray (aka Murray Techman) began his dancing career in 1912 when at the age of seventeen, he won a Waltz contest. That same year, he invested two hundred dollars in dance lessons from Vernon and Irene Castle, afterward declaring himself publicly as a professional New York City dance teacher. In 1925, he began teaching dance lessons by mail order which included written explanations and step diagrams of popular dances of the time (Stephenson & Iaccarino). Thirty years later, his business had grown into a chain of franchised studios throughout the United States. Eventually some five million Americans would register for home social dance lessons and learn the Arthur Murray Method of ballroom dancing.

Murray's special contribution to American dance was in the 1930's with the creation of the "Magic Step." Murray's "Magic Step" is said by Nick Enge to have been originally introduced as "the Collegiate Swing." Quite possibly the greatest dance step ever invented, Murray continued its development from "all slow walking steps" to syncopated rhythmic movements like "quick-quick-slow (QQS)," a rhythm originally proposed by Anna Slezakova in 1834 (Tango "The Greatest Dance Step Ever Invented"). This was the supposed basis for the "magic" in Murray's "Magic Step" and his wildly popular American style dance syllabi.

I was unable to obtain first editions of all of Murray's books; however, I was able to personally obtain and read the following:

In his 205 page, *How to Become a Good Dancer* (1942), Murray discussed in detail Waltz, Fox Trot, Tango, Rumba, Conga, Samba, La Varsovienne (or "Little Foot" based on the Schottische), Jitterbug and Lindy Hop.

In his popular 125 page, stapled pamphlet, *Let's Dance* (1953), he mentioned Waltz, Fox Trot, Rumba, Mambo, Tango, Swing, and Samba. In it, Murray also included a section on dance exercises, as well as briefly introducing the concepts of interpretation and variation. In another stapled pamphlet, *Murray-Go-Round: The Arthur Murray Dance Book* (1958), Conga appeared in place of Mambo, and Jitterbug for Swing. It is in *Murray-Go-Round*, Arthur Murray explained, "After 25 years of teaching dancing I made an astounding discovery. Believe it or not, 75% of all popular steps are merely variations of this one very easy step." This pattern, based on two slow and two quick steps is the foundation of the Arthur Murray style.

In his 254 page, 1959 edition, Arthur Murray, in his book *How to Become a Good Dancer,* published what could be called one of the early American-style syllabi. It included American Waltz (11 figures), Fox Trot (9 figures), Tango (5 figures), Rumba (6 figures), Cha-Cha (4 figures), Mambo (6 figures), Merengue (5 figures), Samba (7 figures), Swing (5 figures) and Rock 'n' Roll (4 figures). Figures were accompanied by timing, rhythm, foot positions, alignment, turn, rise and fall, poise, hold and sway with limited information on foot rise, footwork (the part of the foot in contact with the floor) and floor craft. In the case of Waltz and Foxtrot, the book included a basic amalgamated routine and an interesting section on how to dance Waltz steps to Fox Trot Music!

Fred Astaire

In 1933, Broadway musical shows and movies began featuring ballroom dancing. The movie 42nd Street was a big hit, sparking a "series of musicals starring Bing Crosby, Alice Faye, Dick Powell, Ruby Keeler, Sonja Henie, Dorothy Lamour and many others" including the incomparable Fred Astaire and Ginger Rogers (Stephenson & Iaccarino). In fact, Bing Crosby, Alice Faye and Dorothy Lamour weren't known for their dancing, though Crosby did dance later in the 1954 film, White Christmas. Dick Powell, Ruby Keeler, Sonja Henie and, of course, Fred Astaire and Ginger Rogers were all accomplished actor-dancers.

According to Bill Adler in his book, *Fred Astaire: A Wonderful Life*, it all began in 1917, when Fred and his sister Adele appeared in the patriotic review, Over the Top.

Performance and show dancer Fred Astaire got his big break dancing with Joan Crawford in the movie Dancing Lady. Later, in 1933, he and Ginger Rogers danced a Tango and Samba in the movie Flying Down to Rio. The following years, they starred and danced in The Gay Divorcee featuring Cole Porter's famous hit songs, "Night and Day" and "The Continental," then Roberta with the hit song "Smoke Gets in Your Eyes," Top Hat which included the all-time hit "Dancing Cheek to Cheek," followed by Swing Time and Follow the Fleet, capped by The Story of Vernon and Irene Castle. As a result of these movies and his growing popularity, the Fred Astaire method of ballroom dancing emerged. In 1936, it was estimated by Donald Grant, then president of the Dancing Teachers' Business Association, that because of the Castles, Arthur Murray, Fred Astaire and Ginger Rogers, six million people were learning social dance in various franchised studios across the USA (Stephenson & Iaccarino).

The Fred Astaire syllabi, first published in 1962 in *The Fred Astaire Dance Book*, edited by Lyle Kenyon Engel, were written specifically to explain and promote "the Fred Astaire Dance Studio Method." In the book, Astaire listed the American Waltz (9 figures), Foxtrot (7 figures), Tango (9 figures), Polka (5 figures), the "Fred Astaire Swing Trot" (5 figures), Rumba (9 figures), Mambo (7 figures), Cha-Cha (8 figures),

Samba (7 figures), Lindy Swing (6 figures) and the Twist ("simple basic" only). Figures were accompanied by timing, rhythm, foot position, foot rise, footwork, turn, poise, hold, sway and included select performance amalgamations and basic demonstration routines. The 1978 version edited by John Monte and Bobbie Lawrence added body movement, including "contrary body movement" and "continuity styling," both further emphasizing quality of movement. Perhaps because of its attention to detail, the Fred Astaire American style is still today often referred to simply as The American Style. Both the Arthur Murray and Fred Astaire American-style syllabi, as originally published, included only one basic proficiency level.

Chapter 2
American-Style Smooth and Rhythm Dance

The Complete Book of Ballroom Dancing is an evolving history of American style Smooth and Rhythm dance. I say "evolving" because there are as many American Smooth and Rhythm figure lists and syllabi as there are dance studios in America.

According to USA Dance Academy, technically speaking, American-style ballroom dance currently includes the Waltz, Tango, Foxtrot, Viennese Waltz (the American Smooth ballroom dances); and Cha Cha, Rumba, Swing, Bolero and Mambo (American Rhythm ballroom dances).

Arthur Murray Studios, on the other hand, list the "Magic Step" Foxtrot, Waltz and variations, Tango; Rumba, Mambo, Cha Cha, Samba, Merengue, Swing and Rock N' Roll, while the Fred Astaire Franchise lists Foxtrot, Slow Touch, Waltz, Tango; Swing, Discotheque, Rumba, Merengue, Cha-Cha, Salsa, Samba, Bossanova and Hustle (Monte).

American Waltz, Foxtrot, Peabody, Tango and Swing/Lindy constituted the "Standard" American-style ballroom dances in the USA around Wold War II. It is interesting to note that while Waltz, Foxtrot (and its quick stepping cousin the Peabody) and Tango are typical "round" ballroom dances of the times, the Swing/Lindy, while popularly danced in large ballrooms, was a "place dance" later relegated to the Rhythm group of American-style dances.

Waltz

In the late 1800s, two special modifications of the Waltz developed in the United States. First was the Boston, a Slow Waltz with long gliding steps, fewer and slower turns, and more forward and backward movement, somewhat like the English Two-step. The second was the appearance of Waltz Hesitations—the "One Step"—which involves taking one step to three beats of music. The Boston almost entirely disappeared during World War I, but is said by Stephenson and Iaccarino to have stimulated development of the English or International-style Slow Waltz.

For me, the basic character of a dance is important. What makes the Waltz a Waltz is, in my opinion, rotation with distinctive rise and fall over the 1-2-3 count danced in slow-slow-slow (SSS) rhythm.

Polka

The polka, originally a Czech farmers' dance with a distinctive "half-step" (fast hop-like shift from one foot to the other), first appeared in American ballrooms after WWII (Stephenson & Iaccarino). It is, however, no longer listed as an American Smooth dance (American Syllabi Step) or included in the American-style competition ballroom syllabi by the USA Dance Academy.

Two-Step/Foxtrot

From roughly 1890 to 1920, the "Two-Step," one of many variations of The Boston, rose to popularity. The "English Two-Step" in particular provided a segue to the ever popular American and International-style Foxtrot (Stephenson & Iaccarino; Albert Franz, personal communique). In fact, when I first studied International style Slow Foxtrot, my coach, Albert Franz began by teaching me the "English Two-Step" later adding progression which transformed it into a recognizable Slow Foxtrot.

Peabody/Fast or American Foxtrot

The Foxtrot, or as it was initially called, "Fox's Trot," was first seen and popularized in New York City Theatre's rooftop Jardin de Dance in the summer of 1914 by vaudeville actor Arthur Carringford aka Harry Fox and partner Yanscri Dolly. *The Complete Book of Ballroom Dancing* decried, "The foxtrot was the most significant development in all of ballroom dancing. The combination of quick and slow steps permits more flexibility and gives much greater dancing pleasure than the monotonous one-step and two-step which it has replaced."

The American Foxtrot was a fast dance incorporating figures from the Peabody and popular, sometimes Charleston-like, animal-named dances. American Fox-Trot has at least three distinctive forms based on tempo: (1) a "slow to medium Fox-Trot for enjoyable [social and beginner] dancing"; (2) the medium Roseland Fox-Trot; and (3) the fastest Fox-Trot, the Peabody. The carriage is erect, knees are soft and there is no motion above the hips (Stephenson & Iaccarino). My competition coach, Mr. Albert Franz, would say that Foxtrot is like ice skating: smooth, "buttery" and one of the most complex and challenging of ballroom dances. According to Stephenson and Iaccarino, the basic characteristics of this dance are (1) multiple rhythms based on the slow-slow-quick-quick (SSQQ) and/or slow-quick-quick (SQQ) rhythm; (2) constant progression; (3) "no motion above the hips;" and (4) the distinctive "brush" step.

Tango

While Stephenson and Iaccarino stated that the basic American-style Tango rhythm is SSQQS, this may be true only at the social/beginner level. In contemporary American and International Tango, the "basic" rhythm is often said to be SQQ and is danced this way even to music from a century ago). In some Tangos (mostly milongas) the rhythm is heard and danced as SQQQ with improvisational adjustments to match the "feel" of the music (Origin).

The two authors of *The Complete Book of Ballroom Dancing* have also stated that, "The hold in Tango is unique, with partners in close contact" with "no daylight" between them. I personally don't agree with the "no day light" part; in fact, a strong left position of the leader and partner are more characteristic, in my opinion. I do agree that Tango is a crisper, more staccato dance, with knees flexed more than other ballroom dances, and without rise and fall. Mr. Albert Franz has characterized it as being like a "stalking tiger."

American-style Tango per Stephenson and Iaccarino has three additional characteristics: (1) a figure involving slowly drawing the ball of the foot across the floor to the supporting foot with no change of weight; (2) a "change stop," both forward or backward, called a corte; and (3) a half turn on the ball of one foot with the free foot held directly behind it called a "fan."

Viennese Waltz

Performance and competition level American-style Viennese Waltz is typically characterized by dramatic extensions; long, sweeping "open" turns; and, due to the speed, less rise and fall than in the slower waltzes (Franz, personal communique).

Rumba

According to Stephenson and Iaccarino, the "true" Rumba was African in origin and limited to the lowest social strata —"the native rumba folk dance is essentially a sex pantomime danced extremely fast with exaggerated hip movements and with a sensually aggressive attitude on the part of the man and a defensive attitude on the part of the woman." In fact, while the Rumba may have had distant musical roots in Africa through abakuá and yuka traditions, the dance, or "Rumba Complex" as it is often known today, likely originated in Western Cuba, the "heart" of both Rumba music and dance being the musical clave "slap" (Penalosa) and dance "break" or change of direction on the sound, respectively.

Son Cubano, sometimes known simply as "Son," was and still is a distinct genre of music and dance that originated in the highlands of eastern Cuba during the late 19th century (Stephenson & Iaccarino). It contained elements of Spanish and African bantu origin. Son Cubano is said to have first reached Havana circa 1919, where the first recordings are said to have been made (Penalosa). After World War II, it became a popular dance of the middle class in Cuba. Slowed, polished and played in cut time it became the American Rumba or "Rhumba." In 1913, Lew Quinn and Joan Sawyer are credited as having first introduced it to the USA (Stephenson & Iaccarino).

In the early 1900s, Rumba Flamenca, one of the palos (styles) of Flamenco, surfaced in Spain. Not truly derived from Cuban Rumba and not a dance in and of itself, it spawned a series of other Spanish styles of "Fast Rumba" music such as Catalan and Galician Rumba. In the 1980s, these styles gained international popularity thanks to the French ensemble called the Gipsy Kings, whose Rumba music is so fast that my partner and I have used it in preparation for Samba performances.

American Rumba, a version of Cuban Son, was acknowledged to have been introduced into the USA in the late 1920s by Xavier Cugat and his orchestra. Starting at the Coconut Grove in Los Angeles, it was featured in sound movies like In Gay Madrid (Stephenson & Iaccarino).

The American Rumba is typically danced in a box pattern, similar to the beginner or "social" American Waltz (Stephenson & Iaccarino). In fact, my partner and I have successfully introduced International Waltz to beginners by first introducing the American Rumba box step to Rumba music, then substituting Waltz music, introducing basic American Waltz figures and de-emphasizing Cuban motion.

According to Stephenson and Iaccarino, American Rumba, originally "Cuban Rumba," is a spot dance whose music comes from drums and claves and is danced to a four-count QQS rhythm.

If there is one characteristic feature of Rumba, American or International style, it is "Cuban motion," a "discrete but expressive hip movement" created by and creating a subtle shift of weight. Interestingly, while Stephenson and Iaccarino point out that "some Latin-Americans appear to resent the United State version—which they feel spoils the dance—American Rumba seems to be here to stay."

In fact, Stephenson and Iaccarino detailed Cuban motion as a discreet hip movement created by bending and straightening the knees with weight transfer. However, I question several statements from the "Rumba" section of their book: First, the statement that it is danced "with flat feet." Cuban Motion is, in my experience, best created using ball-flat rather than flat footwork. Second, "shoulders remain quiet throughout dance." Once again, in my experience, a strong shoulder lead is necessary for the partner to anticipate the next figure (the dance, without shoulder movement would also, I think, appear decidedly adynamic). Third, "the woman maintains an erect and proud carriage" seems to me to go against the romantic character of the dance. I would prefer to say that the woman maintains a "provocative, sensual attitude" throughout the dance. Fourth, my coach, Mr. Albert Franz, has always emphasized three basic movements that, for me, underlie all others: the Rumba Walk, Spiral and Hip-Twist. Stephenson and Iaccarino don't mention any such steps or their equivalents. Finally, American-style competitive ballroom dance syllabi generally include a much slower version called Bolero, not mentioned at all by Stephenson and Iaccarino (American International Dance Association).

Bolero

Bolero is a slower, more sensuous, romanticized form of Rumba, emphasizing open figure work and lines, appearing more in contemporary American-style performance and competition syllabi. Bolero incorporates, in addition to Cuban motion, contra body movement (CBM) and Waltz's rise and fall as found in the some American Smooth dances (Bolero).

Mambo

The Complete Book of Ballroom Dancing mentioned, "In the back country of Haiti, the mambo is a voodoo priestess;" but "there is no folk dance in Haiti called the 'mambo'." Instead it attributed Cuba as the origin of the dance "where there are substantial settlements of Haitians and it is entirely possible that there was some voodoo influence behind the name."

More likely, it originated as we know it today, in 1930s Havana, where charangas (an ensemble that plays Cuban dance music) incorporated elements of popular Latin dance genres like the Son Cubano (Mambo Music Guide).

Ballroom Mambo as we know today is attributed to Perez Prado, who popularized it at La Tropicana nightclub in Havana in 1943, and later in New York's Park Plaza Ballroom (Stephenson & Iaccarino). The jerky movements and violent acrobatics of early Harlem Mambo illustrated in the 1952 film The Spirit Moves have slowly changed to what we know today as Mambo.

During the 1950s, Tito Puente, then at the height of his popularity, helped to bring Afro-Cuban and Caribbean Mambo, Son, and Cha-Cha to dancers across the USA, as demonstrated in the 1955 Italian film Scandal in Sorrento in which Sophia Loren dances "Mambo Italiano" with Vittorio de Sica (Sophia Loren).

Mambo experienced a revival in 2010 with the appearance of Eddie Torres and His Mambo Kings Orchestra and All Star

Dancers (Eddie Torres) and again in 1987 with Patrick Swayze and Cynthia Rhodes' Mambo in Dirty Dancing (Dirty Dancing - 2 "Mambo").

Cha Cha

The word "cha cha" is said to be derived from the name of a small seed pod used to make a rattle called a che cha which is used by a music leader to create the Cha Cha "beat." In 1953, the Cuban Orquesta América, a charanga orchestra founded in Havana in 1942, presented a lighter, slower version of Mambo music to the delight of frustrated Mambo dancers (Orquesta América). Adding a chassé movement, it created a triple hip undulation in the vein of Lindy, and the Cha Cha was born. By 1959, dance studios are said to have reported that Cha Cha and the International style Cha Cha Cha suddenly became THE most popular social dance (Stephenson & Iaccarino).

American-style Cha Cha is basically a fast offshoot of the Rumba with a Lindy triple step (chassé). An interesting debate surrounds whether to begin the basic step on the first or second beat. In the American-style it can be the first or second beat. In International-style it is always the second beat. According to the authors, much of Cha Cha's popularity is largely based on its metronome-like "ticking" beats (Stephenson & Iaccarino).

I find Cha Cha a dance most easily interpreted as a fun, teasing, flirty dance. Assuming American Cha Cha is, in fact, derived from American Rumba, I will have to disagree with the authors regarding the same five points I mentioned regarding the American Rumba above.

Samba

Stephenson & Iaccarino stated in *The Complete Book of Ballroom Dancing*, that two Brazilian folk dances, the Maxixe (prounounced ma-shish') or Tango Bresilien, and the Samba made their way into American ballrooms starting in 1910, at least partially due to the influence of Vernon and Irene Castle. Unfortunately, the Maxixe was not easy to learn.

What did "take off" was Samba. "The ballroom samba or carioca was derived from the rural 'rocking samba'" enjoyed in Rio de Janeiro. The dance was popularized by Fred Astaire and Dolores Del Rio, dancing the carioca in Flying Down to Rio and several years later by Carmen Maranda, dancing the Samba in That Night in Rio (Stephenson & Iaccarino; Flying Down to Rio; That Night in Rio). Samba, like Rumba, Bolero, Mambo and Cha Cha is considered a true American ballroom dance as it travels counterclockwise around a dance floor. Characterized as a "moderately popular ballroom dance," Samba is, however, "limited pretty much to advanced ballroom dancers because of its speed and difficulty" (Stevenson & Iaccarino). Technically, its difficulty is due to seven different rhythms as well as coordinated forward and back rocks, foot "cuts," abdominal squeezes and releases, and unusual syncopation (Tsuchiya). Personally, it's one of my favorite dances.

East Coast Swing

On 12 March 1926 when the Savoy Ballroom opened its doors in New York City, its first act featured an impressive block-long dance floor with a raised double bandstand. Consistently providing the best in fast Swing-jazz music of the day, Stephenson and Iacarrino reported that dancers quickly developed a colloquial, athletic, often highly acrobatic style. Anything goes as long as it has "that swing," swing loosely meaning a subtle up-and-down pulsation in 4/4 time.

It is important to note that in 1927 a second "Savoy Ballroom" opened in Chicago with a similar venue (Savoy). Again, in 1969, a Club Savoy opened in San Francisco, offering a nightclub, saloon, 40s and "Savoy Style" dancing. It was also one of the nation's first women's nightclubs. The Savoy discreetly catered to female clientele who frequented the club to dance and socialize with other women. In the 1970s, Club Savoy moved to the city of Sunnyvale and in 1976, to its current location in Santa Clara (Sher).

In 1927, following Charles Lindbergh's flight to Paris, a local dancer named Shorty George Snowden is said to have referred to the dance as "Lindy's Hop." Today, the Lindy Hop, or just Lindy (also known as Swing, Jitterbug, Rock 'N' Roll and Jive) is still highly popular. Lindy is currently danced in syncopated two-step chassés accenting the offbeat followed by a break or back step.

By the end of 1936, the "Lindy" had swept the United States, and later, under one of its most popular names, "Jitterbug," it rapidly became an American pastime. Clarke and Crisp noted that during World War II, it spread like wildfire to every part of the world eventually acquiring the name, "East Coast Swing," its formal American Rhythm name. It was subsequently reinterpreted in England by ISTD into the more rigorous and upbeat International Jive.

The American Waltz, Foxtrot, Tango and Viennese Waltz have generally constituted the "Standard" American Ballroom dances in the USA as of World War II, while the American Rumba, Bolero, Mambo, Cha Cha and Swing have generally constituted the "Rhythm" Ballroom dances (USA Dance Academy).

Why call American-style Standard and Rhythm dances taken together "ballroom" dances? Waltz, Foxtrot, Tango, Viennese Waltz and Samba are typical "traveling in the round" ballroom dances. While the Rumba, Bolero, Mambo, Cha Cha and Swing, are "place dances," they are still performed on a ballroom floor.

Merengue

The Dominican national dance, the Merengue, is typified by Cuban motion, using a forced, released leg drag or "side step chassé." It was originally danced to QQ rhythm at a fast tempo. American ballroom Merengue is danced with the same rhythm but at a slower tempo. Merengue was introduced in the USA in the 1950s, but is not a competitive American-style Rhythm dance. It is, instead, a wonderfully fun and easy Rhythm dance appearing mostly on social dance cards (Stephenson & Iaccarino).

Bossa Nova

The Complete Book of Ballroom Dancing stated that the most recently introduced Latin dance is the Bossa Nova, a Brazilian Samba Cancao infused with American Jazz. The dance is said to have reached its popularity in 1962 with songs like "The Girl from Ipanema" and "Blame it on the Bossa Nova." However, I must say that, since beginning my dance career, I have never danced Bossa Nova, perhaps because it was never admitted to the American Rhythm or International Latin-American competition syllabi.

Rock-And-Roll

Some have claimed that Rock and Roll (Rock 'N' Roll, Rock 'N Roll or Rock N' Roll) was first introduced to the general public in a 1934 motion picture called Transatlantic Merry-Go-Round featuring Jack Benny. However, this seems to me unlikely. While the phrase "rock and roll" did appear in the movie, I found nothing that could be called Rock and Roll dance. The same can be said of Stephenson and Iaccarino's claim regarding a 1937 song entitled "Rock It for Me." While the lyrics may contain the words "rock and roll," the music was, at best big band slow swing (Chick Webb).

Another mention is from a 1954 radio show, "Rock 'n Roll Party," in fact, "premiering in 1952, 'Bandstand' (as it was originally called), began life as a local program on Philadelphia-based WFIL, which broadcast both radio and television programs." It also "featured local teenagers bopping to the current hits of the day" (Brady).

Most would agree that in 1954, when Elvis Presley released "That's All Right," the era of what is thought of as contemporary Rock and Roll music and dance officially began (Varga; Elvis Presley).

For me, the 1954 Bill Haley and the Comets' recording, "Shake, Rattle, and Roll" and 1955 "Rock Around the Clock" were not only top records of the year, but all-time Rock and Roll music to which I still dance International-style Jive today.

By the 1950s, people were watching television programs like Dick Clark's "American Bandstand" featuring a wide range of Rock 'N' Roll fads including East Coast Swing, West Coast Swing, Jive, Jitterbug and Be-Bop, most being versions of the Lindy (Rock & Roll). It was from Dick Clark's American Bandstand that "sock hops" came about and my competition coach, Mr. Albert Franz, began his career. No mention of radio or television dance would be complete without also mentioning Lawrence Welk's orchestra which included dancing to a variety of dance musics including Swing on Saturday nights for an unprecedented 27 years—the longest prime-time musical program including dancing in television history (Gorman).

Twist, Disco and Hustle

The 1960s Rock and Roll era saw several more new American dances appear, including the Twist, Disco and Hustle, all wildly popular for a brief time. These 'couple' dances (that interestingly no longer required physical touch) quickly lost popularity during the 1970s (Stephenson & Iaccarino).

Chapter 3
International-Style Ballroom Dance

Ever since people began dancing, they have sought to record their movements, first in oral form, later in pictograms, writing and more recently digitally. These records are a way to preserve a particular dance and allow one to reproduce it at will; this and perhaps a desire to record a particularly impressive dance for posterity and take one's place in immortality.

Big American-franchised dance studios were training millions of dancers in their unique American figures and styles of dance. Each studio was also peddling their own dance notation system. In Europe, however, British dance teachers were scrambling to come up with one, cohesive European notation system. On 25 July 1904, the Imperial Society of Dance Teachers (ISDT) was formed in Covent Garden, London. Later, in the early 1920s, primarily in response to the many divergent dance figures being developed in the USA and brought to Europe by American soldiers, Philip Richardson, then editor of The Dancing Times, called a series of informal conferences of teachers of dance. By 1924 separate branches of ISDT, all of which later became faculties, were established. In 1925 the society officially changed its name to the Imperial Society of Teachers of Dancing or ISTD as it is known today. Its stated purpose was to bring order to the world of ballroom dancing (ISTD "Discover Our History").

Having officially created a Ballroom branch, a committee of five ISTD dance teachers were chosen to write a single, internationally-recognized list of syllabus steps. The committee, according to Clarke and Crisp, included Josephine Bradley, Eve Tynegate-Smith, Muriel Simmons, Leslie Humphreys and Victor Silvester.

Basically, the committee reviewed, reinterpreted and re-assembled the ballroom dances into a single shared style, called the "British" or "International" style. This approach was reflected in Alex Moore's 1936 *Ballroom Dancing*, including the concept of basing the figures on "natural walking movements." Note: I was unable to locate the 1936 edition; however, in the 1939 Fourth Edition and 1986 Ninth Edition both "International" and the "natural walking movements" concept appear. Even so, the "natural walking movement" concept-statement per se does not appear in The Imperial Society of Teachers of Dancing's 1994 *The Ballroom Technique* Tenth Edition. The "natural walking movement" is described in considerable detail in the 1986 edition under THE FORWARD WALK and THE BACKWARD WALK: With the feet parallel and the man leading the woman in close embrace (the man typically moving forward and his partner moving backward), the man directs her progress across the ballroom floor.

The committee eventually worked out syllabi for the a set of "standard" (now called "Ballroom") dances. In 1948, The Imperial Society of Teachers of Dancing's *The Ballroom Technique* was first published, summarizing and enlarging the standard syllabi to include visual elegance.

According to ISTD, the primary intent was to notate, codify, elaborate and "perfect" these standard dances. What resulted, however, was an "International-style" of ballroom dancing. This new style would be taught from a single set of syllabi by dance teachers all over the world, the exception, of course, being the USA (ISTD "Discover Our Mission"). ISTD selected the Waltz, Foxtrot, Tango and Quickstep, developing their own versions of these popular American dances based on natural walking movements. These dances were organized into syllabi with specific figures that were to be taught and mastered in a fixed order by academic fellows, dance masters and student teachers. The dances were further adjusted so they could be danced to popular tempos of music like ragtime and Charleston.

These International-style ballroom dance syllabi emphasized the timing, rhythm and footwork of each individual dance and figure under the rubric "Technique." Musicality and expression were introduced later. To these four International ballroom dances, the United States' branch of ISTD—USISTD—later added the "modern" Viennese Waltz (USISTD International Viennese Waltz).

These International-style ballroom figures were codified by Moore without proficiency levels. They were later reorganized by ISTD and USISTD into a single, consistent set of dance syllabi by proficiency level now recognized throughout 90% of the world. ISTD and USISTD proficiency level figures were determined to be Basic (Student Teacher), Associate, Standard (Licentiate), and Named Variations (Fellow) levels. This is quite different from contemporary International-style competition, where competitors compete within Pre-novice, Novice, Pre-Championship and Championship levels. These last proficiency levels correspond directly with emerging World DanceSport proficiency levels (Tsuchiya).

ISTD versions of *The Ballroom Technique* used largely English-language-based descriptions typically limited to three-figure amalgamations, along with "precedes" and "follows" based on the proficiency level of the dancer. The descriptions often proved difficult for newcomers to use unless one already knew the basic movements and figures involved. Nonetheless, this style of syllabus dance notation and choreography became quickly and firmly entrenched.

Reynolds in his book *Ballroom Dancing: The Romance, Rhythm and Style*, related that after dealing with standard dances, ISTD-qualified teachers quickly began to organize the various Latin American (notated as Latin-American) dances. In 1951, ISTD officially created a Latin American branch and five ISTD dance teachers were chosen to write a single, internationally-recognized list of dances and syllabus figures. This committee included Sydney Francis, Doris Lavelle, Doris Nichols, Dimitri Petrides, Elizabeth Romain and Peggy Spencer (see Lavelle). This list was collated and edited on behalf of the Committee by Elizabeth Romain and Peter Pearson and resulted in ISTD's *The Revised Technique of Latin-American Dancing*. Basically, the committee reviewed, reinterpreted and reassembled the Latin-American dances into a single common style—again designated the "British" or "International" style.

International-style Standard and Latin-American dancing differed from the start. According to ISTD's *The Revised Technique of Latin-American Dancing* (herein called ISTD's *The Revised Technique*), the basic Latin-American hold is more complex, including not just closed and close facing positions, but also fan; promenade; counter-promenade; fallaway; right side-by-side; left side-by-side; right shadow; and right and left contra positions. The overall visual effect is that instead of "two dancing as one" in a single fixed frame, there is a constant give and take of power exchanged often with the dancers dancing in open frame. ISTD's *The Revised Technique* addresses this variety of frames, but not the characteristic "gooeyness" associated with give and take of power. I had to learn the later from Albert Franz.

The International-style is danced by several magnitudes more dancers than the American style. ISTD's *The Ballroom Technique* and its distinctive notational system, originally a series of foot pictograms and photos, remains to this day firmly based in the English language. However, a slowly growing set of standardized abbreviations began appearing as evidenced in the 1994 Tenth Edition used as the reference work for this book. These are currently used to describe: (1) the various positions of the body in relation to the feet, e.g. contrary body movement position (CBMP), promenade position (PP), and outside partner position (OP); (2) alignment of the feet in relation to the room; (3) turn, measured as foot-turn usually in eights of a circle, e.g. 1/8 turn to the right; (4) rise and fall (elevation and lowering that is developed through the feet, ankles, legs, torso, neck); (5) footwork [the part of the foot in contact with the floor, e.g. heel (H) or toe (T)]; (6) sway (inclination of the body away from the moving foot and/or towards the inside of a turn); (7) frame (poise and holds); (8) syncopation (the deliberate disturbance of a regular timing pulse or accent); (9) preceding and following figures, all with reference to (10) counterclockwise movement in a grand circle down a line of dance (LOD).

Today, most DanceSport competitors and coaches use some version of the ISTD ballroom notational system. Figures are often given abbreviations, like NST for a Natural Spin Turn, and are nowadays described in the dancer's native language (e.g. ISTD's *The Ballroom Technique* is also available in Japanese, which, being Japanese, I prefer to consult).

This system, archaic as it may seem, is fueled by an almost universal ban on videotaping at performance and competitive, including DanceSport, events. On the other hand, four new DanceSport notational systems are beginning to appear: One is the result of the growing demand for video-based instruction. For example, Dance Vision's Learn to Dance with the Champions series of instructional movies (now called "Vintage DVDs") with complete, pre-scripted video practice routines and visually choreographed performance and competition routines. The second is based on recent attempts to digitize, integrate and computer-analyze silhouette-style graphic dance recordings. A third follows on the heels of computerized special effects cinematography. A fourth, mid-COVID-19, is based on the need for an entirely new, safer infrastructure for performance and competition. This future one is needed to address an increasing consumer demand for virtual reality-based entertainment, teaching and instruction.

Each of these "new" forms of notation are progressively richer and at the same time more technologically complex. Which, if any, will emerge dominant is, at this time, anyone's guess. My inclination is that the latter, if developed to the point that one could perform and compete "by distance" would change contemporary dance notation and usher in a new era of richer, more robust dance notation.

Currently, one big hurdle for all DanceSport notation systems, including ISTD's *The Ballroom Technique* and *The Revised Technique* is that there are usually six to twelve couples on a social or competition dance floor. Each couple must constantly modify pre-scripted movements or choreographed routines to avoid couple-couple interference (called "ungentlemanly conduct," a disqualifying criterion in some competitions).

Fundamentally, International-style standard (now ballroom) dances are *partner* dances, according to ISTD, generally danced in a stylized, closed position. For example, the lady's right hand is placed in the gentleman's left, her left hand on his right shoulder. His right hand is place behind her shoulder blade, or, in the case of Tango, on her lower back (ISTD *The Ballroom Technique* 1994). This creates a single, shared, vertical center-of-balance for each partner to use in his or her movements. In my experience, this single, shared, vertical center-of-balance is reflected in what some competitors now call a Unified Top Line. Albert Franz, repeatedly says to always focus on Top Line. If Top Line—which includes frame—is correct and consistent, most of Moore's footwork, sway, and foot position "Technique" is said to happen naturally. Another way of saying this is that learning dancing often begins with the feet and ends with the Top Line.

Progressing on, "First and foremost, partners typically work to show off the female, or in some cases, the following partner's flexibility and suppleness" (Tsuchiya). Men, generally the leader or initiator, are expected to at least create the appearance of leading. Initiators therefore have a considerable amount of intellectual as well as kinesthetic "technique" material to acquire. This is especially true at the initial or Basic level, early in training. The initiator must at least know how to clearly signal a particular figure or phrase, so the follower can complete it. The follower's goal is then to showcase a particular expressive interpretation (Tsuchiya). ISTD doesn't directly address this. Instead it creates the foundation for creative expression and provides a notation system, under one inclusive title, "Technique."

Followers must develop the strength and stamina to allow the initiator's apparent power and control to be fully and seamlessly expressed (Tsuchiya). This is done by moving and building on the initial power movement. The best dancers allow the power to visibly course through the body using connection and follow-through. Unfortunately, this entire issue is also not directly addressed in either Moore's *Ballroom Dancing* or in ISTD's *The Ballroom Technique*. Instead, ISTD lists several mirror image Basic dance figures. Later, at the Associate and above level, ISTD documents the increasingly specialized roles of the leading and following partners. It is important to remember that Moore's *Ballroom Dancing* as interpreted by ISTD was always meant to emphasize figures "based on natural movement and walking steps" (Clarke and Crisp). In fact, *The Ballroom Technique* beyond the Basic level, can be thought of more as a detailed list of *unusual* Waltz, Foxtrot, Quickstep and Tango movements, steps and figures, which increase in number and complexity with level.

On the other hand, Albert Franz said during a coaching session that in competitive DanceSport, improvement requires being aware of movement details and slowly eliminating or replacing those that do not enhance the couple's natural movement appearance with ones that do. In this sense, ISTD provides, mostly by implication, a helpful reference list of "faults," by dance, that, if not enhancing a couple's appearance or movement, should be eliminated.

My partner and I try to cultivate a common or visual sense of inner feeling and emotion. It is from these inner feelings that the transcendent nature of dance emerges. Mr. Franz often reminded us that no one wants to know how achy I feel, only that I appear to be moving in concert with the music, my partner and the audience's expectations. In essence, ISTD in *The Ballroom Technique* addresses minimal physical elements, but not necessarily the heart of dance, namely musicality and expression.

Dancing in closed, close frame brings up issues of individual differences in physique, natural timing and movement quality. For example, I am only five feet tall, while my partner is five feet six inches. I have short arms, nearly the same length as my legs; he has long arms and short legs. My partner has a particularly broad chest that creates a wide, strong-appearing frame that I find challenging to fit, given my petite physique. Yet again, people often say my partner has natural rhythm, while for me, Western rhythms have never felt entirely natural.

Finally, my partner likes to make broad, sweeping movements involving lots of extension, whereas I tend to enjoy minute precision. On the other hand, my partner dislikes memorizing complex routines. In short, he loves musical expression, surprise and variation, while I love perfectly executing a movement, exactly as I have memorized it in rehearsal. In dance competitions, however, we are typically judged not only on how well we perform individually but together. We want to appear to do what we do with ease as one. When successful, we invariably want a record of our movements so that we can repeat them. Moore and ISTD offer little advice on these important issues, but they do provide a consistent method of ballroom dance notation.

Slow Waltz

In their book, Stephenson and Iaccarino reported that international-style ballroom dancing probably started with the Waltz. Waltz, from the German verb *waltzen* meaning to turn, roll or glide was born in the alpine regions of Austria and danced socially in the suburbs of Vienna.

Beginning around 1830, Franz Lanner and Johann Strauss the younger introduced the Viennese Waltz, a faster version played at about 55-60 bars or measures per minute (mpm). This led to development of the *Valse a deux pas*, or the Waltz with two steps danced to three beats of music. By 1900, a typical dance program was three quarters Waltzes and one quarter all other dances combined.

According to Alex Moore, a beginner should begin learning Waltz with the Quickstep. The Quickstep walk, quarter turns and natural turns are commonly considered the simplest dance movements for most people to recognize and perform: "The beginner who enters the ballroom with just a knowledge of the Walk, Quarter Turns and Natural Turn in the Quickstep, and Closed Change, Natural Turn, and Reverse Turn in the Waltz, will be able to take part in about three-quarters of the average dance programme."

The International-style Waltz time signature is 3/4, indicating three beats to a measure or bar with a quarter note getting one beat (ISTD *The Ballroom Technique* 1994). According to Franz, it has typically eight bars to a musical phrase. ISTD's *The Ballroom Technique* doesn't list a dance tempo for International Slow Waltz; however, USISTD on its website, "International Waltz" mentioned an approved competition tempo of 28 to 31 mpm with the first beat of every bar accented.

The Ballroom Technique (1994) by ISTD designated Waltz rhythm as all slows, "each step = 1 beat," later notated "S." The leader's footwork generally involves transferring weight from heel to toe on the first beat (1HT), to the toe on the second beat (2T) and from toe to heel on the third (3TH) with late rise and fall. Waltz, in general, is a dance of turn and sway, emphasizing these kinds of basic details (ISTD *The Ballroom Technique* 1994). I've danced the Slow Waltz in a small area, the repetitive three steps being danced in a "box" fashion.' I've also danced Slow Waltz as a continuous walk. However, according to ISTD's *The Ballroom Technique* (1994), the correct progression is a Closed Change to a Natural Turn to a Closed Change to a Reverse Turn moving along the line-of-dance (LOD). This tome also addresses CBM and sway. According to Mr. Franz, more experienced dancers are also aware of, address and record in the more advanced ISTD figures pivots and pivoting actions, heel turns and heel pulls, CBMP, as well as special syncopated rhythm.

Slow Waltz has six named "compulsory" figures (called "Student Teacher" level), ten "Associate" level, eight "Licentiate" level and six named variations at the "Fellow" level (ISTD *The Ballroom Technique* 1994). These are commonly used in DanceSport competition as the core of a Waltz routine. Of all the listed figures, I regard the Natural Spin Turn when done to perfection, as most representative of quality Slow Waltz. In addition to ISTD's 1994 listing of Slow Waltz techniques in *The Ballroom Technique*, there are tens more "Popular Named Variations" (Moore *Popular Variations*) as well a potentially infinite number of individual unnamed variations. Reynolds stated that at its highest level, Slow Waltz is a dance of enticing, sensual pleasure with a veneer of aristocratic composure. While ISTD's *The Ballroom Technique* (1994) provided some of the fundamental elements necessary to achieve this, it is far from comprehensive.

This book also lists at the end "Additional Figures" which, for the Waltz (aka Slow Waltz) include at the licentiate level the Drag Hesitation and at the fellow level the Fallaway Whisk. These figures, while not considered part of the standard Waltz syllabus "may [still] be danced in Medal Tests and in the practical section of Professional Examinations." Personally, I don't favor the Drag Hesitation. For me, it appears adynamic to a less experienced audience. The Fallaway Whisk, on the other hand, is an amalgamation of a Fallaway and a Whisk, which together appear, in my opinion, very dynamic and can be particularly interesting to both new and experienced audiences. In addition this combination is generally unexpected. As far as difficulty, it is a variation of the Fellow-level Fallaway Reverse and Slip Pivot with the Slip Pivot being replaced by a Whisk. I particularly like this amalgamation.

Slow Foxtrot

In *The History of Dance*, Mary Clarke and Clement Crisp described the Cakewalk, a high-stepping African-American vaudeville dance popular in the late 1800s.

Stephenson and Iaccarino claimed that the Fox Trot by name, was first danced socially in the Garden de Dance on the roof of the New York Theatre. It was based on a high stepping trot to ragtime music made popular by Harry Fox, which people later called "Fox's Trot." Wishing to capitalize on this, management introduced the dance with Cakewalk elegance upstairs.

The Foxtrot (aka Slow Foxtrot or Slow Fox) is undoubtedly the most significant ballroom dance of all time. According to Stephenson and Iaccarino, its combination of quick and slow steps permitted more flexibility and greater dancing pleasure than the monotonous one and two-step dances. It is said that there is more variety in the Foxtrot than in any other ballroom dance. Because of this, it can be, technically speaking, the most difficult of ballroom dances to fully master.

Like Waltz, three variations developed: There was a slower version, danced at about 40 mpm nicknamed the Peabody. The other was danced at over 50 mpm. This second version was particularly popular in England, where the ISTD in 1924 assigned it the name "Quickstep." Clarke and Crisp added that the Quickstep is actually a combination of fast American Foxtrot elements and the American Charleston.

The third version, the "Slow" Foxtrot, is perhaps the most danced and versatile of DanceSport genres. The time signature is 4/4, indicating four beats to a measure with a quarter note getting one beat (ISTD *The Ballroom Technique* 1994). There is a major accent on the first beat and, as I typically dance it, a minor accent of the third beat. According to Mr. Albert Franz, further accent on the first beat of every second and ninth bar defines a distinctive eight-bar Slow Foxtrot dance phrase. According to USISTD, International-style Slow Foxtrot music is typically played at 28 to 30 mpm (International Foxtrot).

The Slow Foxtrot rhythm consists of countless amalgamated variations of the basic quick-quick-slow (QQS) rhythm where, according to ISTD, the S foot placement and weight transfer can typically take an entire two beats of music. Slow Foxtrot when danced in long phrases allows for considerable variation in footwork as long as top line rise and fall fit the phrases (ISTD *The Ballroom Technique* 1994). Franz has stated that competitive Slow Foxtrot is actually a flat dance of *illusory* rise and fall created solely in the moving partner's ankles, as with the Feather Step and Three Step amalgamation sometimes called the "Feather in Three" (ISTD *The Ballroom Technique* 1994). This makes the overall effect reminiscent of ice dancing. Slow Foxtrot is characterized as a gliding dance with not infrequent toe-toe steps and a strong sense of linear progression. In fact, the Feather complex is so representative of Slow Foxtrot that the above work listed seven "Feather" variations: Feather Step, Feather Finish, Feather Ending, Hover Feather, Feather Step Commenced in Outside Partner, Curved Feather and Back Feather. Of all the listed figures, I regard the amalgamated "Feather in Three," when done to perfection, as most representative of quality Slow Foxtrot.

According to ISTD's *The Ballroom Technique* (1994), with experience, any Foxtrot that is played slowly can be danced with a distinctive early ankle rise, strong CBM/CBMP and buttery smooth HT rises as inferred in the Feather Step and Feather in Three amalgamation. Together, gentle TH "falls," heel pulls, brush steps and pivots with a distinctive late ankle rise and fall, as well as complex timing and beat values give the dance a dreamy, smooth, floating-on-ice or airy quality. In general, I dance Slow Foxtrot with visibly less body turn than in most of the other standard dances.

Slow Foxtrot has five named "compulsory" ("beginner" or "Student-Teacher" level figures), three Associate level figures, eleven Licentiate level figures and six named Fellow-level variations as listed and detailed in ISTD's *The Ballroom Technique* (1994). According to Albert Franz, at its highest level, Slow Foxtrot is a dance of balance, control and perfect complimentary partnership dancing, giving the illusion of "dream-dancing." While it can be one of the most challenging and difficult of the ballroom dances, its presentation, when done to perfection, is incomparable.

Quickstep

Clarke and Crisp described Quickstep as the British equivalent of the American fast Foxtrot with Charleston variations. International Quickstep is aptly named, being danced at 48 to 52 mpm (USISTD). Like Slow Foxtrot it uses 4/4 timing with four beats to a measure (ISTD *The Ballroom Technique* 1994). Quickstep however has a distinct accent on the first and third beats of each measure. *The Ballroom Technique* suggested that Quickstep phrases can be quite variable but at advanced levels are typically four bars (16 beats) in duration (ISTD 1994). Quickstep rhythm is highly syncopated and therefore quite variable. It consists of figures (many actually amalgamations of simple one and two-step movements) danced in SQQ, SQQS, SQQSS and SQQSSS rhythm (ISTD *The Ballroom Technique* 1994).

Generally speaking, Quickstep footwork uses early but

slow rise over three steps followed by quick but gentle lowering in one step, giving the feeling of rising up a roller coaster hill and then free-falling down (ISTD *The Ballroom Technique* 1994). Reynolds stated that the second and third rising steps are taken on the toes to create an illusion of "body flight" that, when fully developed, is the competitive signature of this dance.

According to ISTD's *The Ballroom Technique* (1994), basic Quickstep progresses with the man moving forward, backward, and laterally along LOD while facing diagonal to the nearest wall. Quickstep, while quite fast, still incorporates CBM, CBMP, HT, and TH actions along with skips, hops, runs and an endless variety of individualized kicks and flicks. In addition to its sixteen named "compulsory" ("basic" or "Student-Teacher/Associate") figures, Quickstep, as specified in *The Ballroom Technique*, has six named advanced "Standard" or "Licentiate" figures (many amalgamated) and five "Fellow" advanced named variations (ISTD 1994).

Alex Moore in *Ballroom Dancing* (Ninth Edition) and Reynolds both agree that as a ballroom expression of jazz, at its highest level, Quickstep is a dance of youthful joy for both dancers and viewers, especially when the illusion of body flight is clearly evident.

A surprise to me was the inclusion in the Quickstep as described in ISTD's *The Ballroom Technique* (1994) of a special Natural Pivot Turn (SQQS) which doesn't appear in any other ballroom dance. Another was the uniquely

Quickstep Tipple Chassé to Right which my partner and I have adapted and danced in Waltz competitions with particular success.

ISTD's *The Ballroom Technique* (1994) lists at the end of the book "Additional Figures" which, for the Quickstep include at the Student-Teacher level the Heel Pivot, sometimes referred to as "a quarter turn to the left [with Heel Pivot]" and at the Associate/Bronze Medal level the Zig-Zag Back Lock and Running Finish, the Cross Chassé and the Change of Direction. My partner regularly inserts heel pivots in the quarter turn to the left for variety. While we have not performed either the Zig-Zag Back Lock and Running Finish or the Cross Chassé in competition, we have used the Change of Direction, again for variety or when "cornered" in competition, a figure adapted from the Waltz. These figures, while not considered part of the standard Quickstep syllabus "may be danced in Medal Tests and in the practical section of Professional Examinations."

Tango

Tango's origins, said Clarke and Crisp, lie deep in Argentine slave dancing, the slaves having come from Africa by way of Cuba. Reynolds stated that by the late nineteenth century, "Tango," probably meaning "touch," had become popular in the slums of Buenos Aires. Dancers there called it barrios con corte, or "slum dance with a rest." Dancers would suddenly pause for a beat or two before resuming.

Early Tango music and dance were widely regarded as obscene. Many Tangos are indeed scandalous, some are still danced by prostitutes to show off their wares to prospective clients.

In the USA, it was the Castles along with Hollywood superstar Rudolf Valentino who popularized Tango with its various sexually suggestive moves (see Rudolph Valentino, TANGO DANCING). It was Valentino, according to Reynolds, who introduced Tango to American dancers. Its popularity was such that in London, many learned it from Gladys Crozier's book *The Tango and How to Dance It*. Popular "Tango Teas" were held in the afternoons at fashionable hotels.

In Europe, Tango was reduced by ISTD to a series of quick head and foot motions, eliminating the more sexualized moves and caresses. According to Reynolds, ballroom Tango today exists in three distinct forms: the International, American and Argentine styles or versions..

By the 1930s, as Clarke and Crisp stated, the "Standard Four" dances—the Waltz, FoxTrot, Quickstep and Tango—were being danced everywhere in the world. Americans, however were continuing to evolve ever more versions of these dances. Today, Americans dance Waltz, Viennese Waltz, Foxtrot and Tango.

Reynolds reported that Tango music, with its 2/4 time signature and all beats accented, is a dance of compelling, driven, demanding character. The official DanceSport tempo is 30 to 32 mpm (USISTD International Tango). Its unusual QQS rhythm with half-beat Qs definitely lends it an air of the unexpected.

The Tango position and hold is low and close, with the woman's position shifted slightly further to the man's right than usual (ISTD *The Ballroom Technique* 1994). This is meant, I think, to convey an illusion of constant body tension. Footwork is based on continuously left-turning strong heel leads without rise or fall. Albert Franz said it has a "stalking character, not unlike that of a tiger slowly preparing to attack."

Alex Moore added that Tango is a dance of "eccentricities" including strong, early CBM and CBMP along with syncopated "links" (sudden body position shifts of the couple's feet and head creating the illusion of a shift of the woman's body to the man's right). Also included are Foot Flicks, to heighten viewer excitement (*Ballroom Dancing* Ninth Edition). Stephenson and Iaccarino identify the Draw, Corte and Fan as additionally characteristic of the Tango. Albert Franz adds that while constantly curving, Tango ultimately progresses along LOD with occasional short, quick phrases danced actually against LOD, again, to produce the unexpected. According to ISTD's *The Ballroom Technique* 1994, Tango routines typically incorporate thirteen basic "compulsory" ("Student Teacher" and "Associate") figures, seven standard (or "Licentiate") named advanced figures, and seven "Fellow-level" named variations to which Alex Moore in his *Popular Variations* adds an amazing additional 52!

One unnamed variation that I like to use involves a quick flick of the head in the opposite direction followed immediately by a quick flick in the intended direction. It invariably catches the audience's attention and makes them think of Tango.

Viennese Waltz

An energetic yet graceful dance, Viennese Waltz is prominent in Alex Moore's *Ballroom Dancing* (Ninth Edition). Listed under the chapter heading, "Popular Dances," it is considered by many to be "one of the most attractive of the ballroom dances and has been a popular Social Dance on the Continent for many years." When "danced in International competitions the Continental [International-style] version of the dance must be used.".

While Alex Moore stated that "There is no doubt that it will now remain as one of the most popular additions to the four standard dances," nonetheless, ISTD does not include it in *The Ballroom Technique* 1994. In fact, Viennese Waltz has always been a favorite part of the four Smooth dances in American-style dance competitions, replacing Quickstep. Currently, it is allowed and in some cases required in some international competitions adjudicated by the DanceSport Federation.

According to Alex Moore, Viennese Waltz is so fast at 56 mpm (*Ballroom Dancing* Ninth Edition) that the international style Viennese dance has only six basic "compulsory" figures: the Natural (right) Turn, the Reverse (left) Turn, Forward and Backward Change figures, Natural and Reverse Fleckerl, and Contra Check (though some would say four "compulsory" figures, two named figures and one or no named variations). In championship competitions, variations are neither expected nor necessarily appreciated. Like Slow Waltz, the time signature is 3/4, however, the first beat is unvaryingly strongly accented.

The hold is similar to the Slow Waltz and Quickstep but the man's left arm is held slightly lower and wider (Alex Moore *Ballroom Dancing* Ninth Edition). In Moore's day, Viennese Waltz had foot rise, however, many contemporary English instructors including my competition coach, English-trained Albert Franz, advocates no foot rise. Even so, at competitions, I am seeing increasing numbers of DanceSport competitors using foot, ankle, body and even top-line rise. This creates a second illusory rhythm of slow, powerful, graceful rotation especially when combined with toe or heel pivots. While some would hold there is less body sway than in Slow Waltz, I find it constant and constantly changing.

I was taught that the man and woman alternately dance the same figures but in different directions, giving the dance the illusion of perfect, yet ever-changing symmetry. Reynolds noted that Viennese Waltz's simplicity of figures makes certain that the most minute technical details receive intense judge and viewer scrutiny.

The Power of Dance

Chapter 4
International-Style Latin-American Dance

The combination of Cuban motion and a "gooey connection" are, in my opinion, the most fundamental characteristics of International-style Latin-American dance. Albert Franz has stated that the characteristic "gooeyness" comes from a "rubber-band-like" connection, slowly stretching open then suddenly and quickly closing or vice versa (Tsuchiya).

The Latin-American dance time signature is typically 4/4 (except that some Samba and all Paso Doble are 2/2 time). ISTD's *The Revised Technique of Latin-American Dancing* (simplified to *The Revised Technique* from here on) further stated that most Latin-American dances have an underlying pulsation; for example, the Rumba pulsation is typically 1-2-3-4. However, one could also count 1-and-2-and-3-and-4-and (called "8-count") or 1-ah-and-ah-2-ah-and-ah-3-ah-and-ah-4-ah-and-ah pulsation (called "16-count"). The book also addressed very simple 4-count "hip, knee, foot" movements. However, according to Franz, at the highest level of International style Latin-American dance, all these movements require attention at the 16-count level. Cuban motion should never actually originate in the knees from a twisting motion, which can be damaging over time, but from movement of body weight forward and backward directly over the ball of the foot, while flexing and straightening the knees. Specifically,

> the hips should move softly from side to side as a result of the flexing and straightening of the knee...every step should be taken with pressure on the ball of the foot with the knee flexed, and as the weight is taken onto the foot, the heel should lower, the knee straighten and the heel of the opposite foot should be released as the hips move softly sideways in the direction of the stepping foot. (ISTD *The Revised Technique*)

In 8-count Rumba, Cuban Motion results more correctly from 1) taking a forward step BF onto a straight leg; 2) slowly releasing the opposite hip; 3) taking a backward step BF onto the opposite leg; 4) slowly releasing the opposite hip; 5) taking a side step BF onto the opposite leg; 6) slowly releasing the opposite hip; 7) taking a backward step BF on the opposite leg; and 8) slowly releasing the opposite hip (Franz, personal communique). The effect imparts a smooth "Figure of Eight" motion to the hips, which, refined further using 16-count, creates the ideal Cuban Motion. To this, ISTD's *The Revised Technique* added a slow 1/8 turn to the L creating a tight, slowly moving circle. This allows Rumba (1/8 turn L), Samba (1/8 turn R), Jive (1/8 turn L), and Cha Cha Cha (1/8 turn L), but not Paso Doble, to turn in a tight circle. Like International style Ballroom dances, which are danced in large "ballroom" spaces, Paso Doble travels counterclockwise in a large circle around the floor, and, according to Franz, high-level Samba travels, in addition to a smaller circle, down the floor in a large counterclockwise manner also (personal communique).

In Latin-American dance, as with Ballroom, "First and foremost, partners typically work to show off the female, or in some cases, the following partner's exceptional flexibility and suppleness" (Tsuchiya). Men, typically the leader or initiator, are expected to at least create the appearance of leading. Initiators therefore have a considerable amount of intellectual as well as kinesthetic "technique" to acquire. This is especially true at the Student level. The initiator must at least know how to signal a particular figure or phrase so the following partner can complete it. The follower's goal is then to showcase a particular expressive interpretation (Tsuchiya). ISTD's *The Revised Technique* doesn't directly address this; however, under LEADS, it says, "Whenever the Lady's steps are not the normal opposite to those of the Man it is necessary for the Man to lead her into position."

ISTD's *The Revised Technique*, GENERAL NOTES explained body and foot positions, alignment, amount of turn, footwork, precedes and follows, abbreviations used, analyses of holds and body positions. Together these create the foundation for Latin-American dancing using the ISTD notation system under one inclusive title.

Initially, The Charts, beginning on page 5 and running through the end of ISTD's *The Revised Technique*, break each of the Latin-American dances into a common set of increasing difficulty levels: Student (Bronze Medalist); Associate (Silver Medalist); and Member and Fellow (Gold Medalist). It is important to note here that International-style Bronze, Silver and Gold do not necessarily relate to the American style Bronze, Silver, Gold, Gold Star and Gold Bar levels. Basically, Student level figures begin with mirrored partner steps and proceed to increasingly different and difficult non-mirrored steps that require increasing partner skills, especially the "gooey" connection with an increasingly evident exchange of power from one partner to the other.

Followers must develop the strength and stamina to allow the initiator's power to be fully and seamlessly expressed (Tsuchiya). This is done by moving and building on the initial power movement. The best dancers allow the power to *visibly* course through the body using connection and follow-through. It is important to note that it is assumed that whereas in Ballroom dancing, the power begins in the legs, in Latin-American dancing, it begins in the upper torso.

Mr. Albert Franz said during a coaching session that in competitive DanceSport, improvement requires being aware of movement details and slowly eliminating or replacing those that do not enhance the couple's natural movement appearance with ones that do. In essence, ISTD in *The Revised Technique* addressed the minimal physical elements necessary, but does not address the heart of dance, namely musicality and expression.

Whereas International-style Ballroom dancing is accomplished in closed, close frame, International-style Latin-American dancing is performed in the twelve different hold and body positions mentioned in ISTD's *The Revised Technique.* This makes Latin-American dancing in the International-style, easier in some ways and much more complex in others. It is easier in that open positions do not require the appearance of "two dancing as one," but more complex in that the following partner be more attentive to subtle leads and power exchanges. This is especially so when an open position leads into a closed position.

In Ballroom, issues of individual differences in physique, natural timing and movement quality are paramount. They are still important in Latin-American dancing; however, connection, especially "gooey" connection, and lead-attentiveness are more important. According to ISTD's *The Revised Technique*, equally important is a knowledge of the normal amount of one's partner's turns.

The idea behind standardizing Ballroom and Latin-American dance and creating specific dance syllabi was that "correctly" trained dancers could dance with other "correctly" trained dancers anywhere in the world. What resulted, however, was that this pressured American studios to organize their various dances into syllabi, such as the Arthur Murray, Fred Astaire, Betty White and countless other studio-based syllabi, incorporating each studio's own proficiency levels.

The Revised Technique by ISTD used largely English-language-based descriptions. My particular edition, 1983, however, included photo illustrations. The photos are obviously meant to assist readers where descriptions proved difficult to use unless one already knew the basic movements and figures involved. This style of syllabus dance notation and choreography changed with future editions of ISTD's *The Revised Technique* where photo-illustrations were eliminated.

A slowly growing set of "standardized" notational abbreviations appeared in the 1974 first edition from which ISTD's *The Revised Technique* evolved. These include (L.) and (R.) for the dancer's left and right respectively; (L.F.) for left foot and (R.F.) for right foot; (I.E.) for inside edge (of the foot); (P.P.) for promenade [pseudo-side-by-side] position and (C.P.P.) for counter promenade position; (O.P.) outside partner position; (C.B.M.P.) for contra body movement position; (S.) and (Q.) for slow and quick movement; (L.O.D.) for line (i.e. direction) of dance; (D.W.) and (D.C.) for diagonal-to-wall or diagonal-to-center alignment; and (B.F.) or (H.F.) for ball- or heel-flat step. Note that nowadays in common use, the periods are dropped.

Franz uses ISTD notation almost exclusively. I use it in a personalized shorthand form in my dance journals to record figures, amalgamations, dance phrases and routines that I want to remember.

While ISTD was busy assembling International-style

syllabi into student teacher, associate, member and fellow proficiency levels, in America, there would eventually emerge one set of syllabi for social dancers and another "stricter" set for "keen amateurs" and performers, and yet another for competitors. America, isolated from the rest of the world, has today as many different American styles, methods, syllabi and performance levels as there are studios and dance organizations. What little they all have in common is the idea of dance syllabi and proficiency levels. In this period of de-globalization, ballroom dancing in the other nine-tenths of the world, led initially by ISTD and now World DanceSport Federation, may soon host many more different regional or continental sets of proficiencies.

Rumba

If ballroom dances by their nature appeal to an older population, then Latin dances appeal to both old and young.

Rumba is said to have originated from Africa. During World War II, the Son, a "cleaned up" version of Rumba, became popular with middle class dancers in Cuba, and with it, Rumba was transformed into "The Dance of Love."

Like its American-style cousin, International-style Rumba's chief characteristic is "Cuban motion," a discreet but expressive hip movement achieved by carefully timed weight transfer from side to side. English or International style Rumba is danced differently. Distinctive forward-and-back steps are used supposedly to de-emphasize the sexually evocative Cuban motion.

International Rumba is a slow, sensual dance of passion and seduction. Mr. Franz has often told me, "Provocative Setsuko! Rumba is a dance of love!" According to ISTD's *The Revised Technique*, Rumba time signature is 4/4 with 4-, 8- and 16-count phrases. Competition tempo is 28 to 31 mpm. According to Franz, emphasis is on the second of the four beats, a split percussive "heart beat:" one, two-two, three, four. In the International style, there is a change of direction just after the split second beat. This, in association with a released or lowered hip, creates a subtle "figure-of-eight" hip motion similar to American "Cuban motion."

The basic hold for most Latin-American dances, including Rumba, is close, closed face-to-face. The man places his right hand on the woman's left shoulder blade, and the woman places her left arm lightly above his curving arm on the top of his shoulder (ISTD *The Revised Technique*). Hold and body variations in International Rumba, including promenade, counter promenade, fallaway, side-by-side, shadow and contra position footwork, are accomplished generally BF without rise or fall. Turns from CBMP are common, sway and CBM are not. "Forward-Weighted Connection" is used to create what Albert Franz described as a "gooey" or "rubber-band" look, slowly building power, then transferring and quickly releasing it to make the dance appear more dynamic.

According to Franz, three basic Rumba movements underlie all others: the walk, the spiral and the hip-twist. It is important to once again make the distinction between a "Figure" and a "movement" (note the difference in capitalization). If a DanceSport competitor has good rhythm, Cuban motion and can execute these three basic movements, he or she will generally command the performance or competition floor. ISTD's *The Revised Technique* stated that there are twelve Student figures, five named advanced Associate figures and seven named Member/Fellow variations. In my experience, there is considerable latitude for technique, especially with regard to torso, free arm and free-hand movement.

International-style Rumba, when well-danced, is almost, but not entirely a place dance. Rather it moves in a slow small circle to the left. For me, the three figures which most typify the International Rumba are the Fan, Alemana and Hockey Stick.

While *The Revised Technique* by ISTD described in detail the execution of a basic Fan, I've found over the years that it is better danced using a particularly quick change of weight on the 4, 1 that positions my body forward to better complete the figure. I also like to sometimes do a "boop"—a pushing back of the hips before changing weight on the 4, 1 that creates an exaggerated change of direction and some syncopation for flair. This can also be accomplished in the Hockey Stick figure.

The Alemana in ISTD's *The Revised Technique*, though considered a Student level figure, is a figure that, in my opinion, can be danced and significantly refined throughout the life of a dancer. For example, in its most basic notation, the Alemana involves mirror image forward, side, back and side movements. In fact, Franz mentioned, but it took almost a decade for me to fully assimilate, that the Alemana, danced with competitive styling is best described as a spiral, hip twist and walk movement in that order. In essence, an outstanding Alemana is actually well beyond Member and Fellow level.

The Hockey Stick, so named because of the directional shape of the lady or follower's 3-Step forward walk followed by a left turn, side and back step, is performed in the shape of a Hockey Stick (ISTD *The Revised Technique*). However, this can appear quite adynamic. Mr. Franz, taught me from the very beginning to dance this figure slightly differently, basically, with a very clear weight change (causing Cuban motion of the hip), followed by five forward steps, followed by a Spiral movement and a step back with clear weight change. This Hockey Stick is quite dynamic and exciting to watch.

While ISTD's *The Revised Technique* described in detail the Closed Hip Twist, the explanation offered is, based on my experience, only helpful if one already knows this figure. The first step for the woman or follower is said to be "R.F. back" with "Up to 1/2 turn to the R. on L.F." Without prior knowledge, one would assume that the woman takes a backwards step onto the right foot. However, it is not possible to turn on the left foot if one's weight is on the right foot. What this must mean therefore is that there is a back movement of the right foot, but the weight remains on the left foot throughout the turn. This is not necessary a "mistake" but one of many examples where the book is more helpful to dancers who already know the figure and are wanting to "brush up" on exactly how to do it according to ISTD. In practice, I personally prefer continuous Closed Hip Twists for surprise, variation and excitement.

The Cucarachas (also called "Pressure Steps") are especially interesting for me as they offer a wonderful chance to show off Cuban motion (ISTD *The Revised Technique*). The Spiral while primarily a woman's or follower's figure, can also be danced by the man or leader for variety. Many men don't like this (meaning they aren't good at it), but my partner does.

Performance Rumba incorporates passion, desire, jealousy, rejection and pain or, as Reynolds summed it: "when a superbly trained and inspired couple dances the Rumba, they act out a personal and complex love story—the man turns the woman toward him, she turns away only to turn back once more and give herself to him before he rejects her…"

Samba

According to Stephenson and Iaccarino, two Brazilian folk dances made their way early into the American ballrooms and Latin dance clubs: the Maxixe and the Samba. Starting about 1910, a variant of the Samba, the Maxixe, or Tango Bresilien, became one of dances favored by the Castles. However, the Maxixe, an excellent interpretive performance dance, proved difficult for social dancers to learn and enjoy.

Samba or Carioca (technically "Rocking Samba") is still widely danced by Brazilians partying in downtown Rio de Janeiro on holidays and at Rio Carnival. It was an easy dance to learn, according to Stephenson and Iaccarino, exuding high energy and considerable sexual power. During Rio Carnival, "schools of Carioca" dance Samba in long processions involving thousands of elaborately costumed dancers interpreting various themes danced to popular Brazilian music. The dance was introduced to United States movie audiences in 1933 by Fred Astaire and Dolores Del Rio when they danced the Carioca in Flying Down to Rio. Several years later, it was reintroduced by Carmen Miranda in That Night in Rio.

The Samba is a moderately popular ballroom dance, limited to advanced ballroom dancers mainly because of its speed and seven different rhythms. Characteristics of contemporary Samba include rapid "cuts" or steps taken on syncopated quarter beats and a pronounced whole body rocking motion and sway (Stephenson & Iaccarino).

ISTD's *The Revised Technique* stated that while Samba music is usually written in strict 2/4—alternatively 4/4—time, the tempo is quite wide ranging from 48 to 56 mpm. Its seven rhythms in 2-, 4-, 6-, 8-, 10-, 12-, 14- and 16-count musical phrases give it the widest range of interpretive possibilities of any Latin-American dance. The basic rhythm is SS; however, there is an alternative basic "bounce" in SaS (slow-ah-slow) rhythm. The five other rhythms include SQQ, QQS, SSQQS

(Franz calls it "Cha Cha Cha" rhythm), QQQQ (Corta Jaca rhythm) and SaSaSaS (slow-ah-slow-ah-slow-ah-slow, mentioned as Volta rhythm). According to Franz, it is best danced in 4-count phrases with an aggregate musical emphasis on every fourth count. This unusual accenting can be further enhanced by a brief whole-body stop or abdominal-ripple-pelvic-tilt motion.

The Samba basic movement and alternative are danced BF (ISTD *The Revised Technique*). Turn, swing and sway are remarkably similar to Slow Waltz (Franz personal communique). What ISTD's *The Revised Technique* failed to mention is that outstanding Samba, like Cha Cha Cha, has a constant, metronome-like tick expressed in the dance by a distinctive, quick pelvic tilt in the half-beat (Franz). While technically a closed hold dance, I've danced the basic figures open, side-by-side and even traveling, e.g. as rotating Spot Voltas. These and particularly interesting leads and follows often require amalgamated "change steps" making Samba challenging even for advanced competitors. Unlike most Latin-American dances, Samba progresses along LOD (ISTD *The Revised Technique*). Nine Student figures, five advanced named Associate figures and nine advanced named Member/Fellow variations are listed.

Regarding the Natural and Reverse Basic, Natural and Reverse Alternative, and Progressive and Outside Basic Movements, ISTD's *The Revised Technique* offered extensive information on footwork, alignment and amount of turn. On the other hand, Samba doesn't seem to me to be Samba without body rise immediately preceding the first step, tightening of the abdominal muscles, pelvic tilt, shoulder lead and where appropriate "wind up" before any rotation. It is these total body muscle movements done in sequence as one in a forward and back rocking movement that Stephenson and Iaccarino called "Step and Cut," and Reynolds characterizes as a "pelvic tic."

Samba walks, like Rumba and Cha Cha Cha walks, in PP Stationary and Side, are not specifically characteristic of this dance, but make excellent precedes to other Samba figures. Again, it is, in my opinion, the inclusion of whole body muscle movement that distinguishes Samba.

Some of the most well-recognized Samba figures are the Bota Fogos: Forward, Backward, Traveling, in PP and CPP, in either face-to-face or shadow position. I like to use Bota Fogos at the start of a series of advanced, new or interesting figures to attract viewer attention and "signal" that something interesting is coming.

Another well-recognized set of Samba figures that are unique to Samba are the Voltas. The Volta movement and figures, while slightly less characteristic of Samba than the Bota Fogos, are, in my opinion, nonetheless an interesting contrast in this dance. ISTD's *The Revised Technique* listed four basic Volta variations: namely, Turning, Traveling, Circular and Spot variations called Basic, Criss Cross, Maypole and Solo

Spot, which can be done face-to-face, or in shadow. I particularly like simple, separated, curving, Traveling Voltas.

The Revised Technique pointed out that certain figures danced in Contra or Right Shadow position will require a foot change (ISTD). Foot changes, while done only by the male partner or leader, are particularly challenging, but are a necessity at Member and Fellow levels. My partner and I routinely incorporate foot changes at the beginning and end of Contra Bota Fogos.

Another especially attractive set of figures begins with the final named variation called the Natural Roll. While not listed in ISTD's *The Revised Technique*, the "Rolls" include the Natural Roll, the Reverse or "Barrel" Roll, which we do face-to-face, and are learning to do front-to-back, perhaps one of the most difficult of rolls.

At its highest level, Samba appears as an intense, electrifying dance of wild physical and often sexual abandon. In fact, it is the result of a highly energetic but disciplined combination of five segmented body movements performed to seven seamlessly interwoven, syncopated rhythms.

Paso Doble

Paso Doble, the fourth contemporary Latin-American competition dance, is danced to characteristic two-beat march music traditionally part of the procession at the beginning of a bullfight. The music used is that of the paseillo, the procession of the toreros into the bull ring, Paso Doble meaning "two step" in Spanish. Clarke and Crisp related that Paso Doble, with its many reflections of bullfighting, is Spanish in origin, but was refined for the ballroom by French dance masters. In an actual bullfight, the torero weakens the bull by using his cape to attract it to participate in well-defined, particularly tiring movements; the matador's role is, quite simply, to kill the weakened bull. Primarily an "exhibition" dance, the man represents the torero and the woman his cape (not the bull as is sometimes claimed). Usually it is the last of the classical competitive International-style Latin-American dances to be learned, due to the high skill-level required to make it attractive.

According to former scrutineer and competition judge, Geoffrey Fells, a Highly Commended Dual Fellow of the United States Imperial Society of Teachers of Dancing in Ballroom and Latin-American Dancing, while:

> the Paso Doble originated in Spain...nevertheless France is where the Paso Doble developed in the ordinary social ballrooms...It then migrated to England...Many of the syllabus figures have French names such as: Sur Place (on the spot); Deplacement (an abrupt movement); Huit (French for eight); Appel (to call - the Matador's call to the bull); Ecart (from the French word 'ecarter' meaning to separate); La Passe (to pass); Coup de Pique...[others] have English names such as: Sixteen (sixteen steps); Link (to join); Chassés (to move sideways); Chassé Cape (caping action using

the Chassés); Fallaway Slip Pivot as well as Open Telemark...And some Spanish names such as: Banderillas (hooked sticks used to goad the bull); Fregolina (the cape being whipped quickly behind the Torero).

Furthermore:

Each figure tells a 'story'. The whole dance tells the story of the bullfight. It is a character dance and it must be danced with great style and great precision of footwork. The bullfight is a matter of precision - precise movements - and is a matter of life and death and this must be portrayed in the dance. The gentleman portrays the Toreador, or the Matador or the Picador. The lady is a Flamenco Spanish dancer and often acts as the Matador' cape (she is never the 'bull').

Note: I had the distinct pleasure of personally knowing and working with Mr. Fells during his years as Organizer and Director of the Hawaii Star Ball.

According to Reynolds, Paso Doble is a dance of posture, the man dancing with the chest held high, the shoulders positioned wide and down, the head inclined forward. ISTD's *The Revised Technique* added that body weight is kept well forward and footwork is mainly BF, although many figures require the dancer to begin with a distinct heel lead followed by a pronounced body weight shift called an Appel.

While formally danced without rise or fall, Albert Franz taught me the use of a slowly "unfolding" coordinated foot-ankle-knee-torso-neck rise to lend the dance a greater sense of drama. While the dance is still popular throughout Spain, it is not easy to find Paso Doble music in strict 2/4 time at 60 to 62 mpm. I know. I've been to Spain in search of music to dance Paso Doble. The best music lends itself to four-count musical phrasing with every fourth beat emphasized (ISTD *The Revised Technique*).

Normally, one step is danced to each beat, making the basic rhythm SS; however, both foot and body movements are often highly syncopated to increase the drama of the dance. Paso Doble, emphasizing as it does action in the bullfighting ring, is theatrical in nature. It is a quixotic dance in which the man, instead of the woman, strikes the dramatic poses using movements, lines, extensions and body-shaping to express the essence of the dance (Reynolds). It is mainly a performance and exhibition dance, so unusual and uncommonly danced at ballroom soirees, that it received only passing mention in Clarke and Crisp's The *History of Dance*, and was not even mentioned in Stephenson and Iaccarino's *The Complete Book of Ballroom Dancing*.

In my experience, CBMP, CBM and sway are commonly used to the extreme. Varying patterns of steps and delayed heel-drops, coupled with complex, sinuous hand and finger movements borrowed from Flamenco, are, on occasion, added to focus some attention onto the female partner. Such movements, however, are generally discouraged in competition.

The Revised Technique inferred that of the Latin-American dances, Paso Doble in particular utilizes Close Closed Facing

Position. The man places his right hand on the Lady's left shoulder blade, the lady resting her left arm lightly on his arm following the curve of his arm to the shoulder (ISTD).

Paso Doble has ten Student, five Associate and ten Member and Fellow figures (ISTD *The Revised Technique*). Figures unique to Paso Doble include Sur Place, Appel, Displacement, Separation, Huit (Cape Passes), Sixteen, Grand Circle, La Passe, Banderillas, Coup de Pique, Fregolina (with and without Farol), and two especially advanced figures, the traveling spins from Promenade and Counter Promenade Positions. Like the actual entrance and bullfight, this dance progresses like Samba, about the room in counterclockwise direction.

The Basic Movement is a series of small forward or backward steps danced on the balls of the feet (ISTD *The Revised Technique*). Mr. Franz taught me to end it with a slow arm extension and sudden flourish prior to an Appel and Separation or Displacement, a "trademark" I use to this day.

Unlike other Latin-American dances, in ISTD's *The Revised Technique*, a Promenade Link in Paso Doble begins with an Appel and is executed with a flourish in CBMP. I like to use it to attract judge and audience attention immediately before or after a traveling figure like a Fallaway Reverse, Chassé Cape, Sixteen, Fregolina with Farol, or the Traveling Spins from Promenade or Counter Promenade Position.

I find this dance particularly fascinating, and would like to aside address some Paso Doble figures that I find of special interest.

ISTD's *The Revised Technique*, Student level figure, Separation, for me, represents the torero dramatically unfurling the cape. It is a syncopated figure that "snaps" like the opening of the cape. If it doesn't "snap," it isn't a separation or unfurling, it's just a series of steps. I like that the figure includes Sur Place. While the book explained that Sur Place is done with "elevation" on step 4 with gradual lowering over steps 5-8, I prefer a slow whole body rise throughout for a more dramatic effect, as if the torero were tantalizing the bull.

The Huit or Cape, another basic Student-level figure, seems to me an adaptation of Separation. To me, this figure represents the torero flourishing the cape from side to side. Like Separation, it includes and also ends with Sur Place. The Huit is the foundation for the popular Sixteen, yet another Student-level figure, the more advanced Associate-level figure called La Passe and The Chassé Cape, a Member and Fellow-level figure. My partner particularly likes The Chassé Cape which we use in our Paso Doble routine choreographed by Albert Franz.

I'd like to also comment on the Fregolina incorporating the Farol, a Member and Fellow-level figure that is most dramatic, in my opinion, representing a grand flourish of the cape with climactic return into his bent arm. This is a "winner's" gesture with all the drama of having escaped death for yet another day.

Finally, I personally like to begin my Paso Doble with a "classic" figure, to my surprise absent from ISTD's *The Revised Technique*: the Salvador. Similarly, I like to end my Paso Doble with another "classic" figure, the Flamingo Steps in Pressed Line. Both of these figures are advanced named variations given to me by my performance and competition coach, Mr. Albert Franz.

JIVE

During World War II, Clarke and Crisp noted that American Jitterbug had begun to spread like wildfire to every part of the world. It was subsequently reinterpreted in England by ISTD into the more rigorous and upbeat International Jive (*The Revised Technique*).

Jive is traditionally last in a "Ten Dance" competition, requiring competitors to reserve enough stamina for what many consider the most physically demanding Latin-American dance.

Jive is, technically, the only truly "American" International Latin-American dance and is closely related to American Swing, Boogie-Woogie, Jitterbug, Bebop and Rock 'N' Roll with elements from Twist, Disco and Hustle (Reynolds).

Stephenson and Iaccarino quoted Duke Ellington as having said that what makes Swing "Swing" can't be easily written into music. Personally, I like to say that Jive is more a feeling than a dance.

According to ISTD's *The Revised Technique*, International Jive has a 4/4 time signature and is danced at a brisk 40 to 46 mpm. The "basic" pattern is two Jive Chassés followed by a Jive Link. However, it is interesting to note that in "the book," the Jive Chassés are not actual figures but presented in prelude under the title "The Jive Chassé." In fact the "basic" pattern according to ISTD's *The Revised Technique* is presented as a Link Rock and Link.

Jive is danced as a three-step Chassé to the man or leader's left (QaQ) to four beats, followed by a three-step Chassé to the man or leader's right (QaQ), followed by a Fallaway Rock (QQ), resulting in seven rhythmic motions in six beats, a truly unusual syncopated pattern. However, I was taught by Albert Franz the more useful rhythm of aQaQ/aQaQ/QQ, resulting in eight rhythmic motions to six beats. This second rhythm honors the musical "connection" that is considered by many as an absolute requirement of good Latin-American Jive.

Albert Franz stated that Jive can be danced in single, double and/or triple-time, creating constant, interesting variation. Jive is danced BF. It has a characteristic quick body rise created by straightening the bent knees—an "up" motion rather than the "down" motion characteristic of American Rock'N' Roll. This action is hard for many to master. Danced in triple time, Jive has a distinctive syncopated Chassé (side, close, side) as part of its basic step and is followed by a back rock, at its highest level performed with Cuban motion. Triple-time rhythm is often denoted aQaQ, where "a" is pronounced "ah," and represents collecting the body onto center, then placing weight into a flexing knee. Then on the "Q," the knee is quickly straightened with body rise to the point that the body can be momentary "off the floor." This most energetic style of Jive lends to fast Kicks and Flicks danced "on the rise," an audience hallmark of performance and competition Jive.

ISTD's *The Revised Technique* denoted only two Latin-American dances that move, like ballroom dances, around the room, and Jive is not one of these. Jive is a lively, rotating, in-place dance in which the partners dance toward each other around a common center. To this, Franz and Reynolds added that while it might not appear such, Jive in the strict sense has both CBMP and CBM. The latter, is a small torso and upper body turn in the opposite direction of the intended turn to gather pre-turn body tension and give speed and precision to the actual turn. The head always follows late. Rocks and Spins accomplished with this connection are part of the expected character of the dance.

Jive has nine Student, five Associate and five Member and Fellow level figures (ISTD *The Revised Technique*).

At this point, I would first like to comment on ISTD's Student-level American Spin (*The Revised Technique*). I think this cheeky spin is of particular importance because (1) it begins with a hand change, and (2) it Spins in a direction that is unusual for the woman or follower. In Jive, like many Latin-

American dances, there are two movements that are particularly interesting in that they "break the rules:" One is a hand change, the other is a foot change. We use a foot change to segue into side-by-side kicks and flicks creating a subtle break in audience expectation.

The Whip, a Student figure, and the Whip Throwaway, an Associate level variation, are of particular interest to me in that they can be performed exactly as indicate in ISTD's *The Revised Technique*, but don't "look right" to audiences without syncopation, which, in my opinion, is a necessary attribute of "Swing."

Another figure of which I'm particularly passionate is the Member and Fellow level Chicken Walks, where partner connection and syncopation are absolutely essential to the character of the figure and dance.

I personally like both Toe Heel Swivels and Flicks into Break. Both are Member and Fellow level figures. Like Chicken Walks, the success of both figures is based on strong hip movements in strong connection. Toe Heel Swivels are an unusual step in competitions, but one I particularly like as it has that special "feel" of "Swing/Jive." Flicks Into Break (and "Kicks" which are not listed in ISTD's *The Revised Technique*) are a signature figure in Jive performance and competition. Almost everyone includes Flicks and Kicks in a Jive routine, and because of this, judging is very strict. One characteristic of the best Flicks and Kicks is when they are performed on the upbeat/rise. Like ballet, there are no "okay" Flicks and

Kicks. They either are perfect or fail to capture judge and viewer interest.

Reynolds admired Jive when danced at its highest level as the best expression of fast, youthful exuberance.

Cha Cha Cha

While American Swing, Boogie-Woogie, Jitterbug, Bebop, Rock 'N' Roll and later Jive were tearing through America and Europe, even when it became well known, many dancers did not seem to care for the American dance called the Mambo. Many ballroom dancers criticized it for having more of the jerky character of social Jitterbug. It had none the smooth movements usually associated with refined Latin-American dance. Stephenson and Iaccarino said that many people found the pause on the first beat with syncopated foot movements roughly on the 2-3-4 to be unnatural. In 1953, a Cuban orchestra named "America" played a modified Mambo with a three note undulation on the fourth or slow count and, voilà, the American Cha Cha was born. By 1959, dance studios reported it to be the single most popular Ballroom and Latin (technically, Rhythm in the American-style) dance, which it is said to remain to this day.

Most Latin dance *affectionados*, both American and International-style, are more comfortable with the International-style Cha Cha Cha (verses American-style Cha Cha) and Samba than with Mambo's unusual rhythm. Also, Cha Cha Cha lends itself easily to quick dramatic styling variations.

And, while some American studios have revised their Cha Cha to begin on the 1, International-style Cha Cha Cha as described in ISTD's *The Revised Technique* and danced by my partner and I, mentions the first foot movement on the 2 beat, substituting instead a hip relaxation on the 1.

Cha Cha Cha is a happy, carefree, "cheeky" dance, considered by some to be the most exciting of the Latin-American group. Basically, it features the dancing couple involved in "flirting." The time signature is 4/4 with 4-, 8- and 16-count phrases danced at a 32 to 34 mpm tempo. This timing is interpreted by the dancer with foot movements on 2, 3, 4 & 1, giving beat value of 1, 1, 1/2, 1/2, 1 (ISTD *The Revised Technique*).

Stephenson and Iaccarino stated that much of Cha Cha Cha's popularity is based on its metronome-like "ticking" beats. It's interesting to note that in ISTD's *The Revised Technique*, like Rumba and Paso Doble, Cha Cha Cha includes no rhythm (S or Q) notation. In a private lesson, United States Professional Latin-American, North American Latin, Latin World Cup, Dancesport World Cup, and Latin World Trophy Champions Tony Meredith and Melanie Lapatin informed me that syncopated rhythmic variations do, however, occur, such as "QQS" and "QQQQ" and are often included to lend further "spice" to the dance.

Cha Cha Cha hold, steps, figures and movements are similar those of International-style Rumba, although they are often executed with a "crisper," earlier transfer of weight. Cha Cha

Cha's signature figure is the Cha Cha Cha Chassé, a forward, backward or sideways movement complex of three steps in which the second step closes on the "and" count, followed on the third step by full transfer of weight. A popular attractive variation, which I like to use, involves a slight crossing action on the "and." This occurs when moving forward or backward. The toe of the back foot is placed near heel of front foot with toe turned out when moving forward, and the heel of front foot being placed near toe of back foot with toe turned out when moving back. The footwork in the forward Chassé is BF, B, BF, while in the backward Chassé it's B, BF, BF (ISTD *The Revised Technique*). This "Cha Cha Cross," as it is sometimes called, is loosely patterned on the popular Member and Fellow level Cross Basic figure. In the Cross Basic, the toe of the back foot is placed near the heel of the front foot with the toe turned out. Otherwise, as indicated in the ISTD *The Revised Technique*, Cha Cha Cha footwork is almost entirely BF. without rise or fall.

Musical expression is quite similar, and often identical to Rumba, as the Cha Cha Cha, while technically a variation of Mambo, is more figuratively a variation of the Rumba. Albert Franz as well as Stephenson and Iaccarino have stated that Cha Cha Cha's twelve Student level figures are based on the three basic Rumba movements described earlier with the possible addition of the Cha Cha Cha Chassé. At its highest level, Cha Cha Cha is often portrayed as a "tease" dance, with the woman presenting her body as the desired object, constantly inviting the man to pursue her.

Three figures which most typify the International Cha Cha Cha are the Fan, Alemana and Hockey Stick (ISTD *The Revised Technique*). I would add to these, the Cha Cha Cha Chassé movement. I have frequently observed that Cha Cha Cha, like Rumba, requires syncopation and "gooey" connection to be effective in performance and competition. Franz often reminded me that four fundamental Cha Cha Cha figures underlie all others: the Promenade Walk, the Hip Twist, the Spiral and Chassé. If a DanceSport competitor has good rhythm, Cuban motion and can perform these eight basic figures/movements excellently, he or she will generally command the competition floor.

ISTD's *The Revised Technique* listed twelve Student level figures, six named Associate level figures and seven named Member/Fellow level figures. In my experience, despite the detail offered, there is considerable latitude for individual technique and interpretation. For example, "the arms should be held in a natural and unaffected way and never be conspicuous" can be interpreted in many different ways. Furthermore, "In many figures the partner is held with only one hand; the free arm is never static and always moving slowly between the following three positions, taking a whole bar of music to do so." In my experience, especially with regard to torso, free arm and free-hand movement, the use of variations of these "techniques" often become deciding factors at competitions.

ISTD's *The Revised Technique* described in detail the two Student level figures, the Three Cha Cha Chas (forward and backward) and the Natural Top, and the Associate level figure the Reverse Top. These two pairs of "opposite" steps are, in my opinion, of equal difficulty level. Changing a figure from one turning direction to another isn't about simple reversal, as such with forward-to-backward or "mirror imaging" situations. The process involves entirely different hand positions, steps, body shape, footwork, and precedes and follows. Going from Natural (right-turning) to Reverse (left turning) Top is particularly challenging, at least for me.

In ISTD's *The Revised Technique*, the Hand to Hand and New York, for example, would appear to spectators as similar figures, just executed in opposite directions. However, the Hand to Hand commences Right and Left, while the New York commences Left and Right. Furthermore, while footwork is the same, the Hand to Hand requires fifteen steps, while the New York only ten. Finally, aside from an Alemana precede, the follows are quite different requiring different skills than simple mirroring. It is this fact that makes Cha Cha Cha steps that often appear to audiences to be mirror-style figures more difficult to do well.

ISTD's *The Revised Technique* listed Time Steps as a Student level figure, but in terms of complexity I would place it higher as, for example, Time Steps include the Guapacha variation (pronounced Whappacha), a syncopated rhythm notated in Cha Cha Cha not in S's and Q's, but in "2 and 3 4 and

1" and called "timing [sic]" rather than the more correct "rhythm." While in their simplest form, Time Steps are "acceptable," they lack the panache of the Guapacha variation, which gives both dancers and viewers more of a feeling of Cha Cha Cha, emphasizing its teasing and coquettish flavor.

I was immediately curious about the meaning of the name of the Associate level figure Aida, essentially one side and five backward steps in Cha Cha Cha "rhythm." There are various theories, two of which include that the name is derived from the name of the Cuban woman named Aida who demonstrated this step to her ISTD visitors. Another is that it was given because it resembled the movement of performers holding hands and retreating at the time of an encore on the opera stage. These and other theories remain. Nonetheless, the Aida in ISTD's *The Revised Technique* involves the man (or leader) and woman (or follower) retreating in a V-shaped position. The Aida is, like so many advanced figures, "like" another figure (in this case the Hand to Hand) but danced in the opposite direction, with different steps, different body inclination, and different precedes and follows.

The Spiral, an Associate level Cha Cha Cha figure, while considered an almost mandatory performance or competition figure by many, is, in my opinion, particularly unique in that the essential Spiral movement is already a part of a Student level figure call the Alemana. Technically, it might be better to learn the more advanced Spiral figure with its inherent Spiral movement earlier in order to correctly perform the Alemana.

NOTE: In ISTD's *The Revised Technique*, the figure called the Spiral begins with a half a basic step followed by a spiral movement.

Rope Spinning, the first of the Member and Fellow level figures, involves ten steps and a cowboy-style overhead Rope Spinning as if to catch prey. My favorite precede is the Alemana, essentially a turn to the right and walk behind the man. "The book" described the figure as a forward walking figure in which the woman or follower is led to turn abruptly to the right. In fact, a better and more consistent explanation would be that the woman is led to walk to the man's extreme right to perform a completed spiral movement and then a Hip Twist to return to face-to-face closed position.

Cuban Breaks, a Member and Fellow level figure in ISTD's *The Revised Technique*, includes a Cuban Break movement that can be used in a particularly wide range of applications in a variety of figures. As a figure in and of itself, it is a modified, syncopated part of the Cross Basic, where, in closed face to face hold, on counts 2 and 3, and 4 and 1, instead of moving the traveling foot forward and back, it crosses in front and then in back of the standing foot. In the Cross Basic, each "cross" is followed by a Chassé. Cuban Breaks can be danced in (1) closed or open face-to-face with hold or no hold; or (2) closed or open side-by-side or shadow position with or without hold. In essence, the first part of a Crossed Basic is danced twice without a chassé to "2 & 3 & 4 & 1" count. Capable of being danced side-by-side or in shadow position, this means that Cuban Breaks as a figure and/or movement can be found in almost every figure in one variation or another, adding considerable variety to the Cha Cha Cha.

A particularly lovely Cha Cha Cha figure, in my opinion is Follow My Leader. This Member and Fellow level figure involves, as the name suggests, the follower following the leader in a 5 bar, 25-step sequence, danced in a figure-of-eight beginning in closed facing position. The couple dances half a Basic Movement, then the man or leader steps forward on the right foot and commences to turn to the right, the lady or follower steps forward on the left foot and commences to follow the man in shadow position. This is continued until the shadow pair complete a figure-of-eight, ending in closed facing position (ISTD *The Revised Technique*). I find coordinated shadow figures particularly interesting because they remind me of Japan, where traditionally, the woman walks behind the man.

According to ISTD's *The Revised Technique*, Foot Changes are not a syllabus requirement. However, while only mentioned in Cha Cha Cha (I have used them in Rumba, Samba and Jive), they open the door to even more complexity and variety. For example, Same Foot Walks. Same Foot Walks require two Foot Changes: (1) from opposite to same foot, and (2) from same to opposite foot, the former typically used to initiate a same foot executed figure and the latter upon finishing. They are solely a man or leader's figure, requiring the elimination of one step in one manner or another. Same foot shadow movements, either done front-to-back or side-by-side are considered by many to be the pinnacle of exciting Cha Cha Cha performance or competition dancing.

The Power of Dance

Chapter 5
DanceSport

From an American Perspective

USA Dance (formerly the United States Amateur Ballroom Dancers Association) created USA DanceSport to administer amateur DanceSport within the USA. As a result a syllabus was published in the *2002 USA DanceSport Rules* as a "list of fundamental dance figures, organized by style, dance and professional level."

In the USA, there are as many dance syllabi as there are major studios. Each has its own particular figure names, descriptions, methods, techniques, characteristics and approaches to American-style Smooth and Rhythm dancing. Perhaps it was their existence, *many with general absence of proficiency levels,* that led the ISTD to form the United States International Society of Teachers of Dance (USISTD) to eventually define a set of American-style teacher syllabi at three proficiency levels, namely, Student Teacher, Associate and Licentiate (American International Dance Association).

As of 2005, the "official" ISTD American-style syllabi include Waltz, (20 figures with 7 variations), Foxtrot (22 figures with 4 variations), Tango (19 figures), Viennese Waltz

(20 figures), Peabody (19 figures), Rumba (20 figures), Mambo (20 figures), Cha Cha (20 figures), Swing (22 figures) and Bolero (20 figures). But do these syllabi actually reflect the continually emerging "American-style?" I don't think that ISTD's American branch, the USISTD, and its American-style syllabi as presented by The American International Dance Association do.

Currently, the majority of American-style competitors compete in America within proficiency levels. Unfortunately, Bronze, Silver, Gold, Gold Star, Gold Bar and others levels of American-style proficiency don't reflect DanceSport-style. This situation is different from International-style competition where competitors compete within Pre-novice, Novice, Pre-Championship and Championship levels which correspond more directly with emerging World DanceSport proficiency levels.

Up to 2004, certification by USA Dance was required of all American and International-style amateur competitors dancing for the USA. Near this same time, the National Dance Council of America (NDCA), the recognized certifying body for professionals, split with USA Dance over control of amateur competition. NDCA published its own amateur American-style syllabi, similar to USA Dance's Amateur American-style syllabi but onerously including over 100 *prohibited* figures, steps and actions at the Novice proficiency level (NDCA).

From an International Perspective

DanceSport by definition is a world sport, first recognized by the United States and International Olympic Committees as an international athletic competitive sport in 1989. Peter Pover, then President of the United States Amateur Ballroom Dancers Association (currently USA Dance), wrote an article entitled "What is DanceSport?" published in the January/February 1999 edition of Amateur Dancer (now American Dancer). In the article, he defined DanceSport as any form of athletic dance commonly referred to as Smooth and Rhythm dancing in the USA. He also included Ballroom and Latin-American dancing internationally that *require specialized athletic knowledge, discipline and muscle development* to perform (Tsuchiya).

DanceSport is now divided into two divisions: Ballroom (Waltz, Foxtrot, Tango, Quickstep and Viennese Waltz) and Latin-American (Rumba, Cha Cha Cha, Samba, Paso Doble, and Jive) loosely following ISTD International-style competitive dance. However, there still remain two different styles, International and American. Both styles are permitted (this is sometimes called "Open" competition versus closed or syllabi-restricted competition). Proposed pre-Olympic proficiency levels have included Pre-novice, Novice, Pre-championship and Championship. It is interesting to note that the "official" World DanceSport Federation syllabus "represents a list of basic figures and actions that may be used in any [WDSF] competition...On a national level the syllabus can be stricter (containing fewer figures). It is recommended that all WDSF member bodies adopt the WDSF Syllabus as their national Syllabus. That would simplify the participation in the international competitions for all competitors in basic categories. The figures in the Syllabus are listed by the name they have in the WDSF Technique Books" (see "Technique Books").

Hopeful couples begin as Pre-Novices and must progress through each proficiency level by accumulating "points" for placing in semi-final round events at recognized local, regional and national DanceSport competitions.

DanceSport, like Olympic events, was initially, by definition, restricted to amateurs. DanceSport, however, is currently danced by amateur, amateur-professional (Pro-Am) and professionals. Initially, USA Dance was the officially recognized certifying body for amateur competitors—called "USA DanceSport Athletes"—as distinguished from National Dance Council of America (NDCA) certified participants. NDCA was the primary certifying body for professional competitors.

Pover mentioned in his 1999 article that the International DanceSport Federation (IDSF) was formed in 1957 to organize member associations at the national and world level (Tsuchiya). IDSF, in turn, recognized USA Dance as the sole certifying body for amateur competitors representing USA in world DanceSport events. USA Dance in return created the United States Dance Sport Council (USDSC) which issued the first official USA DanceSport rule book. Under the rules of the IDSF and USDSC, a recognized DanceSport competition must be officially sanctioned by a member organization of the IDSF and/or World Dance and Dance Sport Council (WD&DSC—the officially recognized International Sports Federation for Professionals). This means that competitors at both USA DanceSport National, Regional and Chapter Championships and NDCA Recognized Competitions could accrue points towards World DanceSport and, by implication, Olympic Competition.

An interesting historical aside was made by Ann Rodrigues in an article entitled "Ice Dance and DanceSport" in the May/June 1998 Amateur Dancers magazine. DanceSport was originally envisioned as analogous to Ice Dance, an established Winter Olympic *partner* event since 1976. Ice dancers use the basic elements of figure skating—use of edges, stroking, speed, smooth turns, posture, balance, partnering skill and fluid motion—to create a choreographed "dance" on ice (Tsuchiya).

It's not an accident that some early DanceSport teachers taught Olympic ice skaters how to dance on ice and were largely responsible for creating Ice Dance, considered by many to be one of the most watched Olympic events. As Reynolds has stated, DanceSport "draw[s] attention to dancing's superb role model of compromise, cooperation, and mutual respect."

Rodrigues further pointed out that DanceSport athletes,

like Olympic ice dancers, must develop both general and specific athletic abilities through rigorous training. Both must perform memorized groups of basic figures as well as respect their partnership and interpret the music in a way that pleases both judges and audiences (Tsuchiya). Both DanceSport and Olympic ice dancing involve both male and female athletes working together as one. Other Olympic sports and dance forms aren't generally partnered or as gender-equitable. As a final aside, DanceSport competitions are judged by the Skating System, a system quite unlike that used for most Olympic sports.

More than 20 years ago in the USA, states began including "ballroom dancing" as an amateur competitive sport in "pre-Olympic games." For example, the Aloha State Games was hosted 13 June 1998 by USA Dance Honolulu (formerly USABDA Honolulu). According to Mr. Roger Izumigawa, former Commissioner of DanceSport for the Pacific Region, ballroom dancing had become a pre-Olympic competitive event. Pre Olympic ballroom dancing was successfully received, with spectators and competitors alike being treated like Olympic attendees (Tsuchiya).

By public demand, the International Olympic Committee (IOC) agreed to pre-trial DanceSport as a potential Olympic sport event by scheduling a DanceSport Exhibition in the 2000 Olympics Closing Ceremony. DanceSport was also featured in the 2002 Olympic Arts Festival held continuously throughout the 2002 Olympic and Paralympic Winter Games.

The International World Games Association (IWGA) consequently agreed to designate DanceSport as a World Game at the request of IOC. World Games are held to honor sports that have full recognition by IOC but are awaiting a slot in the Olympic program.

The Sixth World Games, held 25-26 August 2001 in Akita, Japan, included both Ballroom and Latin-American World DanceSport competitions. Competitors represented 28 of the 73 countries participating in the World Olympics. DanceSport has since become a regular event in the World Games, held every four years, since 1997.

The major effect of DanceSport has been to redefine ballroom dance competition, moving it away from any particular syllabus style. At present, though organized along the lines of ISTD's International-style, USA DanceSport has stated that "basic" figures need be neither defined nor compulsory. Sanctioned DanceSport competitions generally reflect this by emphasizing "Open" competition.

The Power of Dance

Chapter 6
DanceSport, Partnership and Exchange of Power

Everyone by virtue of being human, has personal power, whether they express it or not. Power, itself, however, is not easily defined. Having become fascinated by dance, I found myself asking why it has the often strong positive effect that it does on people. What is this "power" exactly?

Power can be defined as the "ability to act or produce an effect;" "capacity for being acted upon or undergoing an effect;" "possession of control, authority, or influence;" "physical might;" "source or means of supplying energy;" and an "agency...used to impart motion" (Merriam-Webster "Power"). Typically, power is expressed by transfer of energy from one place or person to another.

Dance can be social, performance or competitive. It can be done as an individual, with a partner, or within a group. I studied ballroom dance beginning with social dance, proceeding to keen amateur, then to performance and lastly competitive dance, but always in the context of a partnership. While the previous chapters focused on different styles of partnered ballroom dance, steps and figures, there is much more to partnership dance. The power of partner dance, in fact, can be almost entirely free of spoken language, styles or syllabi, substituting instead physical touch, connection and the constant transfer of energy from one partner to the other.

Being free of language is, in itself, a powerful attribute.

Dancing is said to have co-originated alongside culture and society, being associated with significant life events like weddings, celebrations and funerals; people attending these events were thought to dance their feelings of happiness or sadness. At such events, people of different countries can dance together and in the process come to understand each other's feelings and cultures better. People often add color in the form of costumes and gestures, passing increasingly elaborate information in the form of tradition from generation to another.

Dance is thought to have been present well before spoken language. For example, not far from my house, the Mo'ili'ili' Community Center holds an annual Summer Festival that includes Bon dancing. Originating in Japan, people of any ethnic or cultural background can join in and enjoy common physical movements to Japanese music without ever speaking Japanese. Participants enjoy the individually felt sensation of seasonal festival dance, communicating with each other through shared movements.

In summary, dance—moving one's body through time and space—is innate to humanity and represents a distinctive form of non-verbal communication—using body movement to convey feelings with timing, rhythm, footwork and gesture. No one wants to forget the dances of their society and culture. Dance, in this sense, is life itself, or stated in a Reichean manner, living through movement of life-giving energy (Mann).

It was in the 1950s that dance first began to be recognized not only as a form of social interaction, artistic expression and competition, but also a highly specialized form of body communication. This idea developed differently on the West and East Coasts of the United States of America, the former under the influence of Mary Starks Whitehouse in the form of "Authentic Movement," and the latter under the influence of Marian Chace and Dance Movement Therapy.

Mary Starks Whitehouse in a 1958 lecture entitled "The Tao of Body" is said to have stated: "Two things about physical movement are striking: One is that movement is non-verbal and yet it communicates…I would almost say, cannot lie." She further explained that whatever a physical body is doing can't be hidden by "words, by clothes, least of all by wishes." In this sense, physical movement can be said to be the most fundamental form of honest expression. In short, "just as the body changes in the course of working with the psyche, *so the psyche changes in the course of working with the body*" (the italics are mine), leading her to conclude that the "core of movement experience is the [felt] sensation of moving and being moved" (Johnson)—an "authentic" exchange of power.

International-Style Performance Dance

Dance partnerships typically work hard to show off the following partner's flexibility and suppleness. Men, typically the leader or initiator, have to acquire a considerable amount of intellectual as well as kinesthetic material.

The follower's job is mainly to receive the initiating signal and power, and seamlessly complete its expression. This is done by moving and building on the initial power movement. The best dancers allow the power to *visibly* course through their body using key skills. These skills in DanceSport are called connection and follow-through. In DanceSport, both partners initially learn and practice mirror image basic dance figures. Later, they incorporate increasingly specialized roles, always appearing as if the two are dancing as one.

Ballet, a largely or at least partially un-partnered dance, is possibly the only other dance form which assigns such highly specific movements to each sex or partner. DanceSport movements in particular are highly kinesthetic, incorporating both an individual and a partnership component, I call kinesthetic interpretation. Kinesthetic interpretation fits well with natural walking movements which are at the very heart of social, performance and competitive DanceSport.

In DanceSport performance or competition, viewers do not know what the dancers are actually feeling, only what they project and the viewers want to see.

On the other hand, a dance where one person always initiates and the other responds, can, after a very short time, become rather lack luster. It is the diversity of responses that contribute directly to depth, interest and dance dynamic: namely the power of dance.

Performing a dance is powerful, but it's transitory. Being able to record a dance for posterity significantly adds to its power since it can be re-rendered indefinitely making it and the dancers technically immortal. Ann Hutchinson Guest, in her 1998 book titled *Choreographics: A Comparison of Dance Notation Systems from the Fifteenth Century to the Present*, noted that most contemporary notational schemes attempt to record dancer movements in terms of body placement in space and time. But a few also record body movement energy, power or force.

Strictly speaking, there are as many different kinds of dance notation as there are dancers, dance organizations, schools, and instructors. Today, three particular systems of International-style partner dance notation have proven most useful in staged performance partner dance over the years: the Benesh System (stick figures), Labanotation (abstract symbols) and personal journaling (typically a personalized combination of the above). Labanotation, being the most complex, I would like to take just a moment to comment here.

Rudolf von Laban in *Shrifttanz* (trans. *Written Dance*), envisioned dance as "movement choirs." These "movement choirs" evolved into a detailed and innovative system of recording movement. Guest, in *Labanotation: The System of Analyzing and Recording Movement*, championed Laban's work and made it readily available to the world. In essence, a central staff is used to represent the central body line with right and left columns indicating steps and leg, torso, arm and hand movements. The shapes of various surrounding block symbols indicate directions of movement. Black, dotted or striped shading indicate power (low, normal or high), and their length, the time duration of movements (and thereby rhythm) (Tsuchiya).

DanceSport Choreography

The World DanceSport Federation "Syllabus" specifically listed basic figures and actions that may or may not be used in "restricted" competitions. Open events are not restricted, and in different nations and event sponsors may add or subtract significantly.

The principal change from American or International-style to DanceSport syllabi is the emphasis on "*sporting* events" rather than the World Dance Council's emphasis on dance as an "art." At this time there are an increasing number of organizations world-wide seeking to establish themselves as the dominant representative of DanceSport. That, and the fact that World DanceSport Federation (WDSF) open events are non-restricted, makes it difficult to characterize DanceSport choreography. However, WDSF emerged from the

International DanceSport Federation (IDSF), which recognized a number of dance syllabi, including *The Ballroom Technique* by the Imperial Society (ISTD); *The Revised Technique of Latin American Dancing* (ISTD); *The Revised Technique* by Alex Moore; *Technique of Ballroom Dancing* by Guy Howard (IDTA); *Technique of Latin Dancing* by Walter Laird (IDTA) and *Technique of Latin Dancing - SUPPLEMENT* by Walter Laird (IDTA). The International Dance Teachers' Association (IDTA) includes within its stated prevue both partnered ballroom and a variety of unpartnered non-ballroom dances. As this book is focused on partnered ballroom dance, I will maintain my emphasis on partnered ballroom rather than dance, in general, relying on the above ISTD references as well as approved WDSF national organization syllabi to generally characterize DanceSport. Being a certified amateur DanceSport competitor in the USA (my partner and I also have competed in Japan under Japan DanceSport Federation rules), I rely mainly on fundamental USISTD and USA Dance syllabi when creating competitive choreography.

Waltz

Sometimes called "Slow Waltz," major "restricted level" figures were originally listed in the 1994 publication of ISTD's *The Ballroom Technique* and have been retained in DanceSport. Reynolds in *Ballroom Dancing: The Romance, Rhythm and Style* agreed that danced in open DanceSport competitions, Slow Waltz remains a dance of blatant romance with a veneer of formal aristocratic composure.

Slow Fox (Slow Foxtrot)

The Slow Fox, according to Albert Franz, began as a flat dance of illusory rise and fall created solely in the moving partner's ankles, making it reminiscent of Olympic Ice Dancing. In ISTD's 1994 *The Ballroom Technique*, Slow Foxtrot was characterized as a gliding dance with a strong sense of linear progression. DanceSport competition allows for an infinite number of new Slow Fox figures yet to be discovered and tested in open competition.

Quickstep

Open DanceSport Quickstep allows for a seemingly infinite variety of amalgamated movements and figures. Phrases and rhythm seem to me purposefully varied to bring in the element of surprise.

In my opinion, DanceSport Quickstep is increasingly emphasizing the illusion of "body flight" which is rapidly becoming the competitive signature of this dance.

Tango

The character of Tango is said by Alex Moore to be "eccentric." However, Moore and Reynolds have also stated that in "open," e.g. DanceSport, competition, this genre is slowly recapturing its early sense of erotic enticement, sexual tension and quick changes in sexual feelings.

Viennese Waltz

Alex Moore has stated that in championship (e.g. open DanceSport) competitions, emphasis remains on perfect execution of the classic six figures, variations being neither expected nor appreciated (*Ballroom Dancing* Ninth Edition).

Classic Viennese Waltz was said to have no foot rise; however, I am seeing increasing numbers of DanceSport competitors using foot, ankle, body and even top line rise, creating a second "topline rhythm" of slow, powerful, graceful rotation.

Rumba

"Weighted Connection" is increasingly being used to create what Mr. Albert Franz described as a "gooey" or "rubber-band" look, slowly building power, then suddenly releasing the power to make the dance more dynamic.

DanceSport Rumba incorporates passion, desire, jealousy, rejection and pain adding ever increasing fast and slow movements to add drama and impact.

Cha Cha Cha

Cha Cha Cha (shortened in the American style to Cha Cha) remains a happy, carefree, "cheeky" DanceSport dance, featuring the couple involved in "flirtation" (Reynolds).

Cha Cha Cha hold, steps, figures and movements

decreasingly resemble those of Rumba, being typically executed with a "crisper," earlier transfer of weight.

Samba

Samba, already incorporating a wide range of interpretive possibilities, has even more in open DanceSport competition, making it appear to me increasingly like Brazil's Carnaval.

Paso Doble

In DanceSport, Paso Doble remains a dance of posture.

DanceSport Paso Doble, emphasizing less and less the action in the bullfighting ring, is, in my opinion, becoming increasingly more theatrical in nature, to the point of extremism. As such, open DanceSport competition lends Paso Doble to even more variation and evolution.

Jive

In DanceSport, the most energetic style of Jive lends to fast foot Kicks and Flicks danced "on the rise," already a DanceSport hallmark of Jive.

If there's one statement I believe can be made in truth both now and in the future, it's that DanceSport has ushered in an era of almost constant change and expansion.

In summary, partnership and power exchange, in addition to youthful athleticism are increasing becoming the hallmarks of DanceSport. As such, having "welled up" from social, keen amateur and pre-DanceSport competitive dance, they are at last "trickling [back] down," reinvigorating the same.

A final word about DanceSport: Albert Franz frequently reminds me that all DanceSport athletes in performance and open competition have a "license in their pocket" to use whatever figures and techniques they wish within the general DanceSport guidelines.

The Power of Dance

Chapter 7
Olympic DanceSport

It is important at this point to remember that DanceSport came into being not on its own accord but as a necessary segue from ballroom dance performance and competition to Olympic event.

More than thirty years before DanceSport was conceived, Norman Martin, one of the founders of USABDA, was already suggesting to the International Olympic Committee (IOC) that ballroom dance be recognized as a world Olympic event (Rodrigues).

In 1996, the Canadian Amateur Dancers Association (CADA) established the CADA Olympic Committee and began publicizing the idea (Stevenson). This began an explosion in public interest in performance and competitive dance that continues to the present.

In 1997, at IDSF's request, the IOC recognized IDSF as the official international representative of DanceSport (Pover). In the USA, states began including "Ballroom dancing" as an "amateur competitive *sport*" at the state level in what were called "pre-Olympic games," for example, the Aloha State Games in Hawaii. The Ballroom dancing competitions in the Aloha State games, the largest and most popular multi-sport competition in Hawaii, began to be hosted locally by USABDA-Honolulu on June 13th, 1998. Ballroom Dancing as a pre-Olympic competitive sport was a great success, with spectators and competitors alike being treated like true Olympic attendees (Izumigawa). I know of this personally, because I was there as a competitor.

Because of increasing public and organizational demand, IOC agreed to test the feasibility of DanceSport as an Olympic Event by scheduling a DanceSport Exhibition in the 2000 Olympics Closing Ceremony. Don Herbison-Evans and his partner, Anna Piper were two of the 1,000 dancers in the eight-minute "Love is in the Air" segment that aired before billions of Olympic viewers. "The energy exchange between us, them [the Olympic athletes], the volunteers alongside them, and the audience at our backs, made a crescendo of emotion that turned the eight minutes into a triangle of dream, fantasy, and reality." (see Paradiseresort).

Because of the success of the exhibition, IOC showcased DanceSport, in the broadest sense, again in the 2002 Olympic Arts Festival held continuously during the 2002 Olympic and Paralympic Winter Games. From February through March 17, the world witnessed some of the finest dancers in the world from dance companies like Alvin Alley American Dance Theater, American Folk Ballet, AXIS Dance Company, Children's Dance Theater, Savion Glover, Limon Dance Company, Pilobolus Dance Theater, Repertory Dance

Theater, Ririe-Woodbury Dance Company and exhibitions of the Navajo Nation that mixed partnered and unpartnered modern as well as ballroom and Latin-American dance and gymnastics (Patrick).

DanceSport was subsequently designated a World Game at the request of IOC because there reportedly wasn't room for any new Olympic events at least until 2008. The World Games (versus the Olympic Games) are held to honor all sports that have received full recognition by IOC but are awaiting a slot in the Olympic program. DanceSport had finally become elevated to a sport, a future Olympic sport at that. As a result, the the sixth World Games, held on 25 and 26 August 2001 in Akita, Japan, included 48 couples in Ballroom and Latin-American DanceSport competition (see TheWorldGames). These couples represented 28 of the 73 countries participating in the world Olympics. DanceSport has since been featured at the 2005 Duisburg, Germany; 2009 Kaohsiung, Taiwan; 2013 Cali, Colombia; 2017 Wrocław, Poland; and the 2022 Birmingham USA World Games (The World Games). Interestingly, the World Games are not amateur, thus further opening the door to professional Olympic DanceSport.

Now it's a waiting game. IDSF, the precursor to WDSF, entered a long-term joint venture agreement with Mark McCormack's International Management Group (IMG). IMG, IDSF's official commercial representative empowered to promote and handle all television, sponsorship and marketing rights, agreed to produce eight major DanceSport competition events throughout the world. On July 25, 1998, the first event was screened by United States' National Broadcasting Company. At the screening, sport journalists were officially introduced to DanceSport and began to write and talk about DanceSport in major *sports* magazines and on the air. It was even scheduled to be covered as a sport by the popular but conservative magazine, Sports Illustrated (Pover).

According to Khor Su Min, new-age, international sports reporter for The New Paper, "Ballroom dancing has got the green light to be included as a sporting event at the Olympics. But it's more than a sport..."

"For better or worse. North American mass media is on the verge of discovering DanceSport and capturing its action, color, drama, sensuality and glamour for presentation to a wide audience...DanceSport cuts across ethnic and cultural lines like virtually no other competitive activity" (Reynolds).

> In recent years, ballroom dancing has been expanding steadily, almost subversively, until it stands poised for an explosion of coverage by mass media...No one who has witnessed competitive dancing at the highest level can avoid the impression that these are both artists and athletes. We are drawn to ballroom dancing, performed at the zenith of ardor and skill, because the participants express themselves in a manner beyond our ability and even, to some degree, beyond our comprehension. They per-

form figures and swirls that move our souls, while we cannot motivate our bodies in the same graceful and abandoned manner. Yet we are dancers all, if only in the theaters of our minds. (Reynolds)

I believe that it is time for DanceSport to officially transform into an Olympic sports event. There are, however, several immediate issues that, I think, need to be resolved in order for this to happen.

First, DanceSport as a sport needs a clear primary sponsor. A variety of dance-related organizations continue vying for the position of singular IOC-recognized Olympic partner-dance sponsor.

Second, whatever primary sponsor and organization comes forward needs to bring to the IOC enough public and corporate interest to fund the sport and event.

Third, the current "skating system" of judging needs to be changed to allow for Olympic-style judging that will at least accommodate first, second and third couple placement.

Fourth, DanceSport needs a clear public identity. Currently WDSF, WDC, ISTD and IDTA have conflicting definitions of DanceSport, some so inclusive as to include non-partnered dance of any and all kinds.

Lastly, the issue of whether DanceSport is, indeed, a true sport rather than just a sport in name needs to be addressed once and for all. This last issue, while obvious to most DanceSport contestants, clearly requires another look at dance as a sport.

DanceSport is World competitive ballroom dancing. It is different from many popular sports that typically involve one person or team competing against others. DanceSport competitions involve one dance *couple*, typically a male-female partnership, dancing to prescribed music and tempo, demonstrating not only proper technique, but also poise, power and floor craft that as a whole interpret and reflect the quality of the music and dance. DanceSport is also different from the performing arts in that it is more primal. Not everyone draws, paints, sculpts, sings or plays an instrument, but everyone moves their body. Even in Wheelchair DanceSport, partners dance together with one or both in wheelchairs.

Marian Chace is said by Chaiklin and Schmais to recognize in dance the importance of rhythm, music and song (but not necessarily costuming and visual representations) in a mostly eurythmic sense in a group context. Chace, one of the pioneers of Dance Movement Therapy, is said to have regarded dance more as a form of communication than a sport or art. DanceSport, however, is much more than a method of non-verbal communication. DanceSport contributes to competitors' flexibility, coordination, balance, range of motion, stamina, muscle tone, strength and posture (Sandel), just a few of the attributes of DanceSport that contribute to the power of partner dance.

Interestingly, DanceSport in the hands of the WDSF, has

already begun transitioning from partnered ballroom dance to include other forms of dance like Show or Stage Dance, Disco, HipHop, Salsa, Para-Olympic/Special Olympic and Breaking, this last not requiring a partner (World DanceSport Federation "DanceSport Disciplines"). "Today, the most diverse dance styles that have adopted a sports-based culture, and that have established bona fide competition structures, fall under the genus name" (World DanceSport Federation "About DanceSport").

Whether expanding its appeal and including non-partner dance and dance-like sports will, in fact, help bring dance to the Olympics is yet to be determined.

There are also, in my opinion, considerable differences between ISTD's *The Ballroom Technique* and *The Revised Technique* as referenced by IDSF, and DanceSport technique.

For example, DanceSport technique in general, emphasizes speed and athleticism. Sometimes, Latin-American DanceSport can seem more like a frenetic acrobatic performance at the expense of musical expression, imparting to all five classic Latin-American dances more of a sense of similarity than difference. In fact, in World DanceSport, figures from any one dance are often used interchangeably.

On the back cover of Picart's *From Ballroom to DanceSport*, the Sport Literature Association remarked that, "The past several years have seen a resurgence in the popularity of ballroom dance as well as increasing international anxiety over how and whether to transform ballroom into an Olympic sport..." Picart further added, "as the choreography, costuming, and genre of Ballroom and DanceSport continue to evolve, these theatrical productions are aestheticized and constructed to encourage commercial appeal, using the narrative frame of the competitive melodrama to heighten audience interest." It's my experience that ballroom dancing, during the current COVID pandemic, has almost disappeared as a social activity, though some performers and competitors have been willing to take the risk of disease and even death to continue DanceSport. Likewise, attempts at "distance" DanceSport events via the internet or other digital means haven't proven technologically easy or vastly popular. In addition, unfortunately, USA Dance hasn't advanced, in my opinion, DanceSport to an Olympic event, but rather regressed it by offering competitive non-partnered forms of dance. High jumps, Toprock, Downrock, power moves and Freezes all add to the feeling of excitement and exoticness while removing previous safety restrictions. Sadly, in addition, Olympic sports, which were supposed to be all amateur, are now almost wholly professional, requiring more and more attention to Olympic coaching, costuming, theatricality, and tightly and perfectly choreographed routines that appeal to commercial advertisers.

Picart began her view of the move from DanceSport to Olympic dance as an "insider-outsider" change in sociopolitical perspective. While interesting, comparing ballroom dance and dancer's bodies with victims of political oppression seems a bit "outside the box" to me. This, alongside her distinctly "professional" perspective emphasizing money, power, fame and winning. Having a decidedly different perspective, this all makes me wonder, is this really what ballroom dance, DanceSport and the Olympics are or should be about? Social ballroom dancers, who are mainly amateurs (meaning they don't receive monetary compensation for dancing) far, far outnumber professionals. Amateur dancers, in my opinion, also make up the majority of ballroom and DanceSport viewers.

In fact, not only are most dancers social dancers, there are a surprising number of social dancers in the world. As of 1999, Bonner and Worthen-Chaudhari estimated there may be as many as 10 million nonprofessional dancers in the USA alone. This, compared to 10,000 professionals. When asked, Mr. Roger Izumigawa, at that time the Regional Representative to USA Dance, estimated there to be about 12,000 social dancers in 15 social dance clubs in Honolulu alone. In December 2019, my dance partner estimated that in Hawaii there were perhaps 120 combined keen amateurs and competitors—roughly one for every 100 social dancers.

Picart insightfully mentioned "special issues" of partner ballroom dance, including lead and follow, muscle memory, feelings and emotions, friendship and love, woman verses man (technically, this should have read leader verses follower), dance differences, lessons, enjoyment and frustration, as well as issues of Pro-Am dancing, single sex dancing, including comfort, power differences between instructor and student, and coaching, briefly, what I like to call the "business of dance."

I found it especially telling that Picart included "power." Power, she claimed, was part of the "magic" of ballroom dance. However, I would say that what makes the ballroom dances "magical" is that two are dancing as one while constantly sharing or exchanging their individual power.

Olympic sports are commonly regarded as exactly that: sports. In order to appear in the Olympic program, an event must first and foremost be a sport. While some marginally regard DanceSport as a "steamy" sport, through Picart's lens, DanceSport is a rhythmic, synchronized, gymnastic, artistic performance more akin to figure skating,"but sport...I don't think so."

According to competitive DanceSport, men and women competitors are viewed and judged as different but equal. It is nonetheless true that in competitive DanceSport, expressly beautiful attire for ladies and the appearance of male dominance remain basic expectations. Competitors and viewers expect this, and judges and sponsors know this.

In DanceSport, and one assumes in Olympic sport as well, skin color, nationality and social class do not overtly determine the "winner" (World DanceSport Federation "DanceSport for All!").

Chapter 8
Gender, Sexual Orientation, Race, Culture and Age

If dancing in its social form is a natural amusement providing enjoyment and exercise, it is now slowly changing from a social pastime to a world-class, competitive sport. This has resulted in extensive research and experimentation. Many of the qualitative characteristics of dance are now being transformed into quantitative elements. The relative contributions of each quantitative component are currently being reapplied to increase overall physical function, performance, training, endurance and reserve.

These are all key aspects of dance, especially partnered ballroom dance as a sport, resulting in improved body protection and preservation, contributing to a person's health, recovery and realization. Where do ballroom and DanceSport stand today?

Having appeared on the short list of contested Olympic sports, and having generated more income than any other contested sport in the 2009 and 2013 World Games, DanceSport as a World sport and future World Olympic event appears promising. However, the World DanceSport Federation posted a 29 June 2015 press release on their website, confirming that DanceSport would *not* appear in the 2020 Tokyo Olympics.

Aside from social appeal, glamour and entertainment value, what is it about dance, partnered ballroom dance and DanceSport that makes them important to individual daily life? I took up social dance, later keen amateur and later still performance and competitive dance, and finally DanceSport. At the beginning, dance was a fun way to maximize my health, retain my passion for life and prevent illness and aging (Tsuchiya). In the process, however, I came to realize that dance, especially couple or partnership dance, also presents unique health and healing attributes of its own. For example, it said to:

help memory and mental sharpness
promote awareness of internal rhythm
encourage good posture and deep breathing
include human-to-human touch
support social connectivity
provide an outlet for curiosity, discovery and creativity
create a pathway for the expression of joy

While writing *In Search of Somatic Therapy*, these particular attributes suggested to me that dance might indeed prove to be an ideal way to prevent physical illness and disease, promote natural healing and prevent some or even many of the effects of aging. In addition, over the years, I have come to believe that in doing so, it might actually serve as a way to maintain mental health, and possibly serve as a complementary or even alternative approach to healing both physical and mental disorders.

If so, it would provide a particularly interesting additional characteristic: It would be language-free. That is, it would be an approach to physical, mental, social and spiritual health that is body (somatic) based rather than mental (psychological "talk therapy") based. This might provide a way for people of different cultures, races, ages, genders, sexual orientations and languages to "communicate" directly body-to-body rather than through spoken conversation and translation. My research has led me to believe the answer is related to the ancient Greek concept of "eurythmy."

Pythagoras is said to be one of the first and perhaps greatest of the Greek philosophers, as well as the father of science, mathematics and, to my surprise, healing music. Pythagoras never personally recorded his theories. However, he is attributed by others after him as having been the first to determine that the pitch of a musical note occurs in proportion to the length of the string that produces it. He's also said to be the first to determine that intervals between harmonious sounds that form chords are based on simple numerical ratios. He's also attributed as having discovered that all things emanate their own unique "vibration" (energy) and that the harmony of these vibrations ultimately determines the physical state of individuals, objects, planets, even the cosmos (Tsuchiya).

According to Emmanuel, the ancient Greeks valued rhythm, and thereby dance, more than anything else. He stated, "With the Greeks the dance was an art much more highly regarded than with us. The philosophers attributed to it a moral influence; they said that 'the dance is, of all musical arts, the one that most influences the soul'." He later stated that "Plato said: 'It is the intermediary between the bodily rhythm and the soul, and it is the dance-gymnastic which teaches eurhythmy'."

The ancient Greeks are said to have incorporated eurhythmy into almost everything they did. They walked, talked, sang, chanted, dressed, birthed, exercised, partied, warred and buried their dead to the innate rhythms of the object, body, activity, culture and seasons.

Interestingly, applied to dance, the concept of eurhythmy was antithetical to the modern concept of "rigorous simultaneity of identical movements, executed by all the dancers, and the symmetrical disposition of the groups of dancers" (Emmanuel). In his classic book, *The Antique Greek Dance*, he further claimed, "The Greeks, on the contrary, evidently cared little for the simultaneity and repetition of Ensemble movements...[being] opposed to juxtaposition of like forms." When I read this, I smiled, thinking that the ancients would have favored watching American-style dance rather than International-style Ballroom and Latin-American dance, and quite possibly World DanceSport and future Olympic dance as we currently conceive it. Perhaps there is something of singular importance in this distinction, necessary for DanceSport to fully segue into a modern Olympic sport event.

The special quality of ancient Greek dance was "a very keen sense of mimetic value, joined to perfect rhythm" (Emmanuel). Perfect rhythm—the Rhythm of the Spheres—was what Pythagoras thought made mathematics, music, people and the cosmos work.

Pythagoras used music, and presumably dance, to heal. Dr. James J. Garber MD PhD in his book, *Harmony in Healing: The Theoretical Basis of Ancient and Medieval Medicine*, mentioned that Pythagoras used movement and music to soothe both people and animals. He goes on to say that Pythagoras is considered by many to be the founder of music therapy. Recognizing the profound affect of music upon the senses and emotions, Pythagoras did not hesitate to influence both body and mind with what he is said to have termed "musical medicine." Today, the American Dance Therapy Association defines Dance Movement Therapy (DMT) as using natural and unnatural body movements, many taken from ancient as well as modern individual, interpretive jazz, and contemporary dance, to treat illnesses of the body and mind (see Gleissner).

At the beginning of the 20th century, archeologists rediscovered ancient Greek vases with depictions of dancing maenad. As these vases began to circulate in Europe, interest in ancient Greece once again resurfaced under the formal name "eurythmy." The Anthroposophical Movement, championed by Rudolf Steiner, reinterpreted eurythmy as meaning perfect proportion in sound, movement, color and design. According to Steiner "eurythmy" [ευ (eu: beauty), ρυθμός (rhythms: rhythm)] represented, among other definitions, perfect, harmonious visual proportion.

In short, while the idea of eurythmy was new to most 20th century Europeans, it actually began centuries earlier, when, two thousand five hundred years ago, Pythagoras already knew that dance was the highest expression of the body, mind and soul. It is said he included dance in the Pythagorean Mysteries alongside music and song. But his most important contribution, I think, was the introduction of the idea of rhythm as a method of physical healing. Interestingly, more than one rhythmic healing element would need to come together in "perfect harmonious order" to be most effective.

Margarete Kirchner-Bockholt, in her 2007 book entitled *Foundations of Curative Eurythmy*, stated that eurythmy is the expression of each human leading a "rhythmic life." Frequently quoting Rudolf Steiner, she roughly divided "rhythmic life" into physical, mental, spiritual and astral rhythms. Within the physical rhythms she included organ rhythms such as breathing (lungs), circulation (heart and vessels), digestion (upper and lower digestive system) and muscular exercise, including stepping, bending and stretching. To these, I would add the female and male procreative rhythms, as well as individual mental rhythms, for example, wakefulness (attentiveness to the environment) and sleeping (inattentiveness to the environment). Kirchner-Bockholt stated in her book that the "characteristic of all rhythmical processes is that they do not go on forever, but turn rhythmically inwards upon themselves." Expanding on her statement, these "life rhythms" can be repetitively cyclical or spiral in nature. Furthermore, spiral rhythms might be inward directed (e.g. consciousness), outward directed (e.g. expression), upward directed (e.g. renewal, gestational or nurturing) or downward directed (e.g. dissolution, aging and death). Of these "rhythms," one that consistently appears central to dance is breathing. The ancient Greeks held that the "psyche"—that which animates the body—is in fact "the breath."

As previously mentioned, dancing can be a powerful method of non-verbal communication. Furthermore, while many argue that language is a form of communication only available to humans, dance interestingly is not. Most, if not all, animals (including humans) dance! They might dance to impress potential mates or fend off attackers. As people (we are, after all, first animals then humans), we can certainly dance to accomplish these purposes. But, in fact, we often break into spontaneous dance to express joy when having a good time.

We can easily find ourselves dancing to catchy songs, even to ones without lyrics. Music adds the rhythm of sound to body rhythm through variations in the length and accentuation of sounds. This creates a new level of richness and diversity of expression—consider, for example, the Nutcracker ballet; a game of "charades;" or a pantomime done by Marcel Marceau. All are forms of dance, albeit unusual ones allowing one to communicate the most complex of ideas and emotions.

People, young or old, move their body. My first competition DanceSport instructor and coach, Mr. Albert Franz, said, "Dancing is movement through time and space. In fact I have expressed feelings of happiness and sadness through dancing using…body movement."

Dance is said to have co-originated alongside culture and society, being associated with weddings, celebrations and funerals.

In summary, dancing—moving one's body through time and space—is innate to humans, and represents a distinctive form of non-verbal communication—using body movement to convey feelings with timing, rhythm and footwork. No one wants to forget the dances of their society and culture.

Mary Starks Whitehouse called this perceptive awareness "kinesthesia," identifying it as a genuine sixth sense. She then asked the question, "Could it be that…we are enthroning the rational, the orderly, the manageable, and cutting ourselves off from all experience of the [real] unconscious…which then take their revenge in the form of an exaggerated, compulsive fascination?"

Marian Chace said that through dance, the kinesthetic sense is reawakened, allowing the body and the mind to heal and further develop. Said another way, through dance, people can rediscover and reawaken parts of their bodies that are not normally felt, do not move or are not readily mentally accessible. In doing so, dancers can recover and heal parts of both their unconscious and conscious that have become dysfunctional. This implies that dance involves "something more" than just body movement, active or passive. Something even more than body communication. It involves relearning to move, and by connecting movements with the felt or kinesthetic sense of movement, authentically communicating, healing and self-actualizing.

According to Chase, dance is a form of communication based on (1) pre-scripted body actions; (2) symbolic movements; (3) empathy; (4) rhythmic group activity. Dance is a way to identify bodily "expressions of maladaptive responses to conflict and pain," and prepare persons to express these emotions. Chace states that dance makes "use of symbolic body action to communicate emotions and ideas that defy everyday use of language" (Chaiklin and Schmais).

Chace was also said by Chaiklin and Schmais to recognize the importance of music, song and rhythm. Dance, however, is, as I've said, much much more. For example, dance also improves flexibility, coordination, balance, range of motion, stamina, muscle tone, strength and posture. These attributes of physical fitness and sports are just a few of the effects of the power of dance. It's important to note that Whitehouse and Chase typically have reported their results in terms of individuals or groups rather than in the context of partnership dance.

I studied dance always in the context of a partnership. I believe there to be even more power embedded in partnership dance. I would emphasize actual body movements of dance partners or partnerships. While, like individual dance, free of spoken language constraints, the partnership approach emphasizes physical touch, co-rhythm and the constant transfer of energy from one partner to the other.

Partnership dance, I believe, empowers dancers and viewers in a myriad of special ways. When I'm tired or depressed, partnership dance can be more effective at readjusting my mental state than medicine. Twenty minutes of dance with my partner, like twenty minutes of running, releases that same flood of natural "feel good" chemicals called endorphins, and leaves me feeling energized and positive, except, of course, when we argue.

Dance—particularly partnership dance—makes dance more interesting to both dancers and others. Social, keen amateur, performance and competitive dance, when done with a partner, feels like a different world. One reason is that partnership dancing at any level requires synchronization and socialization. Dancers learn a certain etiquette, sometimes called gentlemanly or ladylike behavior, creating a set of international internal ground rules, opening the door to positive social relationships.

For dancers in general, dance also invokes self-re-creation and self-fulfillment–using one's body to create art, accessing and advancing inner and outer beauty and strength.

For the partnered dancer, it further involves exchanging energy and the creative spark with one another.

In today's world of conflict, dance promotes individual spiritual growth and, in partnership, enriches dancers with shared spiritual knowledge. By spiritual, I mean self-realization of the power within, and its connection to or source from something greater. Humans are not only physical and mental but also spiritual creatures. As such, humans can recognize and even delight in shared spirituality through dance with another.

Partnership dancers learn to recognize the limits of their improvisational skills, which constantly awakens one partner to the other's perceptions. This helps the individuals and the partnership to learn, think and act in new, socially appropriate ways. Partnership dancing provides physical and mental refreshment and relaxation. Through shared laughter and fun, dancing can be personally entertaining as well as provide entertainment to viewers.

A point I personally find interesting is that partnership dancers typically share inspiration and motivation, particularly if they lose themselves in the dance. Partner dancers often mention eventually attaining a feeling of exhilaration "even better than sex." Keen amateur partnership dancing encourages both partners to trust, create, join together into, and encourage the development of deeper social relationships. For example, my partner and I recently had the opportunity of competing in Japan, opening new social horizons for us at various dance studios there. Through these associations, we have made new international friends and developed new long term relationships. This, in spite of my partner not speaking Japanese! Words are not as important as they often seem.

It is of special importance to remember that social Ballroom and Latin-American partnership dance is originally based on natural walking movements. They, in essence, promote appropriate physical fitness, which, especially if begun at an early age, creates a foundation for lifelong health and fitness, confidence, self-esteem and appropriate personal expression.

Dancing encourages dancers to more fully "inhabit their bodies." In accomplishing this, they become more aware of bodily needs, care and limits. Such issues as individual and partnership range of motion, coordination, strength and endurance, typically end up exceeding those of many other physical activities. But perhaps the most important aspect of the power of partnership dance is how it can act as a social "glue." Dancing is an intimate form of social enjoyment that not only brings people closer but creates a shared bond, again, a fundamental aspect of being a human.

Dance, for example according to Picard, is a performing art, alongside music, opera, theatre, musical theatre, magic, illusion, mime, stage monologue, puppetry, circus arts, cinema and performance art. According to Comte, archeological sites depict dance in 9,000-year-old paintings in India, and in Egyptian tomb paintings dated 3,300 BC, suggesting that well before the invention of written languages, dance was a way to impart human information and emotion as well as history from one generation to the next.

The ancient Greeks devoted whole books to music, vibration and dance elevating dance to what they called "eurythmy," including dance in therapeutic healing.

American-style Smooth and Rhythm dances as well as International-style Ballroom and Latin-American dances are the children of this legacy. Both styles are immensely popular socially, and have been elevated by performance and competition to specialized art as well as sport forms. It is my understanding that while they still aren't commonly used for healing, in fact they can play a critical role in contemporary Dance Movement Therapy and, more recently, Somatic Therapy (Tsuchiya).

Gender/Sexual Orientation

Ballroom dance and DanceSport as well as Olympic Ice Dance involve male and female athletes working together as one. However, Rodrigues specifically pointed out that many Olympic sports are individual events, typically divided into men's and women's sports, and aren't in the general sense, gender-equitable. In fact, men's and women's Olympic events are often judged on different criteria, especially when they involve required elements.

On the other hand, social movements have begun pressuring competitive events to become more gender equitable, for example, allowing LGBTQ+ contestants to compete, including in partnered events.

Even more interesting, most Olympic events are language-free. This provides a way for people of different genders to "communicate" to each other, judges and audience using body language rather than spoken language. In deference, some might find this more stressful including, as it can, actual physical contact. For the moment, I would like to focus on the future DanceSport athletes: children.

Social interaction and physical touch between two children, as well as the need to discuss and cooperate together, are invaluable to developing a healthy body and mind. Children, despite their gender, don't "naturally" learn communication, friendship, cooperation and teamwork. They must learn through experience to share and negotiate in a non-threatening way. At its highest level this involves both learning and practicing empathy. Empathy, even in childhood, requires a sense of how another's actions affect their ability to perform, and what they can and can't do in a partnership to be the best they can.

Children, especially, often think of this challenge as one of learning how best to "make friends." Another advantage to dance for children is learning how to interact equitably with other ages and genders.

Moving back to adults (though clearly DanceSport includes children which it is assumed Olympic sport would also) to "win" in the world of DanceSport as well as World

Olympics, generally requires a certain acknowledgment of the "radicalized" form of the sport. While outliers always exist, they may "shake up" but typically won't satisfy judges' or audience' inherent expectations especially regarding gender norms. Gender expectations are rarely written down or "set in stone," except where they present a danger to the dancer, athlete, judges or audience (Picart). It is in regard to this particular concern, that "appropriate" gender interaction is most important.

In her book, Picart discussed "special" issues of partner ballroom dance including lead and follow, muscle memory, feelings and emotions, friendship and love, leader verses follower. That translates into dealing with different physical, communication and learning styles, especially regarding enjoyment and frustration. Pair-dancing, especially same sex dancing may involved differences in manner of contact, comfort and power expression.

It was as a student at an Arthur Murray Dance Studio, that Picart related becoming acutely aware of the challenges of the "follower" role, leading her to state, "Woman, regardless of the level of expertise of the men, were expected to follow the man's lead, even if the man was dancing completely off-beat..." To this, I would add, or completely without a lead.

While true, this confuses the fact that "leading," in my experience, involves initiating rather than controlling or dominating. Likewise "following" isn't necessarily about rigidly doing the leader's bidding. Again, in my experience, it's more about completing what's been initiated in a pleasingly expressive manner. In higher level dance, it is the forward moving partner, male or female, who "leads" and the backward moving partner who "follows;" hence, it's not necessarily a gender issue, but more one of movement direction. As Captain Barbossa pointed out in the popular movie Pirates of the Caribbean, "the code is more what you'd call 'guidelines' than actual rules" (QuotesDisney). In contemporary American society, one could easily mistake "lead and follow" for what Picart and others might consider "gender politics."

Picart then discussed what I call the "business of dance." "It is a business [studio dancing]. One can never forget that," concluding in the end that gender differences where money is involved, can create gender, race and class issues. I found it telling that, in the end, Picart ultimately linked such differences to power. Power, she claimed, was part of the "magic" of ballroom dance. What, in my opinion, makes ballroom dance "magical" is that two are dancing as one, constantly sharing power irrespective of gender differences.

Picart additionally stated that she used "Langer's view" such that "virtual emotions" are "intimately entwined with other issues" such as gender politics. This assumption was used to interpret dance in movies, videos and photographs. Sadly, this assumption is based on the belief that emotions and feelings are one and the same.

However, in my experience, emotions are distinct from feelings: Technically, emotions are actually unseen circulating body chemicals called hormones which call up general behavior sets; whereas, feelings are the response of smooth or "gut" muscles to physical stimuli or chemical emotions (Tsuchiya).

In addition, I have to challenge the concept of the phrase "virtual emotions" (what is a "virtual" emotion?). Also, it is a far stretch to say conclusively that emotions, powerful as they may be, and feelings, are entwined with issues such as gender politics. That is, they may be, but aren't always. In fact, when dancing, I personally am constantly aware of my musculature and thereby my feelings. No one else knows what my emotions are at that time. The same can be said for "partner emotions" (technically from an audience viewpoint, these are observed "feelings"). On the other hand, partner feelings, often "palpable" during dance, also create shared empathy between dancers, as well as between dancers and viewers. While I don't share Picart's opinion regarding "emotional" power in dance, there is no question that dancer feelings can strongly affect dancers and viewers, irrespective of gender.

Gender and power are not, in my experience, as definitive as Picart seemed to assume. Picart's experiences are heavily based in cabaret and theater arts, in which lifts require one partner to be heavily muscled and physically more powerful. I also don't think that it necessary to compose a dance routine based on non-gender discrimination. It is generally better to simply dance well.

Picart turned to cinema in her search for discrimination involving gender and sexual orientation. Both the Japanese version of Shall We Dance? and the American movie, Dance With Me were supposed examples of such discrimination, both being about ballroom competition within a studio context, where, in her experience, gender and sexual prejudice are assumed present. I agree and disagree. They were reportedly apparent in studios where *she* took lessons and later taught. However, I have spent twenty years in studios taking lessons from myriad professionals, and haven't experienced such discrimination. I felt that, for example, she missed the broader understanding of Shall We Dance? From a Japanese perspective (I am Japanese), Shall We Dance? is not about gender, race, eroticism, sex or class discrimination. Japanese thinking is much more indirect. Japanese value the nuances of excellence in discipline, devotion and action. Many of the cultural, gender, race, class and nationality issues she discussed are simply, in my mind, a product of caricature based on cinematic technique used to create dramatic tension through mystery and suspense, a technique for which Alfred Hitchcock, for example, is well known (Bose; Indie Film Hustle). An actress as well as a dancer, I think this distinction is important. Are movies like these more documentary or more "Hollywood-style entertainment" in nature? A similar question remains about dance, whether performance or competitive, is "real," "authentic" dance more than social, DanceSport or Olympic sport in nature?

Another issue for me is the difference between technical complexity and brilliance, and "chickenskin" in performance as well in competitive DanceSport. I found the dancing in The Tango Lesson which Picart analyzed and I watched, brilliant, but the movie never gave me "chickenskin." That is, it didn't have that which transcends dance from "figures on the floor" to something ethereal even "better-than-sex."

The extensive use of movies and films as examples of ballroom dancing, performance, competition and DanceSport is, in my opinion, at best, oblique. That is, that while films may be, though are not always, based on "real world" stories or problems, they are, in essence, works of fiction at best. Citing works of fiction as examples of real world issues, such as culture, race, gender and national bias is "shaky at best."

"Dance turned into genuine sport at the beginning of the twentieth century, when French entrepreneur Camille de Rhynal and a group of superb dancers added the competitive to the social, and when they converted ballrooms into the venue for their contests." The result is that DanceSport, according to WDSF, "has become an all-encompassing brand for an activity that is uniquely accessible and sociable, allowing participants to improve physical fitness and mental well-being, to interact, and to obtain results at all levels...dance transgresses all barriers of age, gender and culture" (World DanceSport Federation "About DanceSport").

Picart pointed out, however, that DanceSport, if it is to become a popular, global, even Olympic sport, needs greatly increased financial support and sponsorship. She ended the subchapter entitled, What's in a Name?: Ballroom or DanceSport? with a summary of the main arguments the IDSF had put forth to "sell" DanceSport as a viable Olympic sport and thereby business. One of the most interesting arguments, in my opinion, is that "DanceSport not only has 100% gender parity, but it is also one of the few sports in which men and women athletes can simultaneously compete against each other on the same surface."

Picart, I agree, correctly stated, "one area remains difficult to conquer: the gendering of ballroom as masculine enough to be considered 'sporty'." Even this, however, can be somewhat deceptive. In my opinion, this means as masculine enough to *men*, women having already accepted DanceSport for its glamour, entertainment, romantic, and, yes, athletic value. DanceSport as an Olympic sport must open the *masculine* door to heavy commercial investment in order to compete as a sports event for full funding within the Olympic organization.

USA Dance, a member of WDSF, plans to make a long overdue change: All their sanctioned competitions are anticipated to specifically become gender-neutral. This means that regardless of gender, competitors are welcome to compete in the role that best suits them and all couples of any configuration will be allowed to compete on the floor together. This change is meant to establish USA Dance nationally and internationally as affording all dancers equality, dignity, and respect (NEWS & PRESS).

As such, USA Dance's Gender Neutral Committee (GNC)

has been crafting a plan for gender-neutral implementation that accompanied a USA Dance motion to WDSF. The motion aims to change the definition of a couple from a "man" and a "woman" to "two athletes" to represent their country at world championships (NEWS & PRESS).

According to the announcement, "The GNC has three primary goals: 1) To craft costuming rules that provide guidance to dancers, while allowing athletes the freedom to express themselves; 2) To establish an adjudicator training session to be held before the 2020-2021 competition season; 3) To work with event organizers so that they can easily make the transition to being fully gender-neutral."

To completely de-genderize ballroom dance and DanceSport, however, would, in my opinion, require doing the same for other "sports," as well as fashion, books, homes, education, medical care—erasing much if not all dimorphic human life. Gender and sexuality issues will *always* be part of any human endeavor, though sports based on two people dancing as one should have fewer such issues. Is it for DanceSport and Olympic sport to singularly resolve these global issues? I think not.

Race/Culture

According to WDSF, dance "transgresses all barriers of age, gender and *culture*" (the emphasis is mine). Ideally, race, which is often embedded within culture, should never be an issue; however, it will remain such as long as nationalism, money and power continue to discriminate.

According to Godel, ballroom dance began and continues to be inseparably steeped in culture. In her view, ballroom dance and thereby DanceSport survives today not by virtue of its distinct cultural contributions, so much as in light of globalization. "The tie that binds all of these dance traditions together is the ways in which they were appropriated and transformed in order to make them more consumable" (Godel). Still, it appears to me that the key is not one or the other, but a *balance* between cultural incrimination and modern day non-discrimination especially in terms of "world" dance.

For example, Godel held that the "incorporation of ballroom into Japanese society provides excellent insight into the ways that the dance form has been used as a tool for socialization, as well as a means of identity construction." Referring to this process as "Japanization" she refered to "…the process in which practices originating outside the country are transformed and molded into a particular vernacular form. This includes cases where practices introduced to Japan are influenced by traditional methods or ways of thinking, and are thus practiced with a vernacular sensibility."

In my mind, the above can be viewed equally as an example or an exception in terms of a World Olympic Dance sport event. Either way, one can't assume that DanceSport as we know it today will end up being the similar to Olympic DanceSport, whatever that ends up being.

Picard talked about gender, race, sexuality, and class discrimination in competitions with regard to dance, costume and even hair style. In fact, she provided many examples, again, mostly from personal experience. However, personal experience, while always true from the experiencer's point-of-view, is not considered as strong evidence, irrespective of the number of reported examples. A group of people witnessing a crime typically describe what they experienced in observing it often quite differently from one another.

Picart went on to say that performance and competition routines typically fail to address concrete and interesting issues dealing with race, class, and sexuality. I agree; however, I don't think that it is necessary to compose a dance routine based on gender, race, class and/or nationality issues. As mentioned before, it is generally better to dance well.

I, for one, fully agree that Olympic DanceSport should be free from nationality; however, as long as the Olympics, by tradition, relates "wins" first to nationality and secondarily to individual athletes, there will continue to be both racial and cultural discrimination.

In this view, discrimination alone is not necessarily "bad." What is despicable is using race or culture as a major consideration in decision-making.

Having said that, it is interesting to imagine how DanceSport, entirely free of race and cultural elements, would actually appear.

Age

Today's digital culture discourages physical activity, especially in children. People today seem to suffer from an inability to relate to living things. Dance, especially when introduced at the toddler age or before, may prove the best way of introducing a love of physical activity and person-to-person socialization necessary to limit the negative effects of today's digital era. And the best way, in my experience, is to convey this by example.

Picart said, "DanceSport is 'nonaggressive' and 'no violence has ever occurred amongst competitors or the audience'." She has also stated that DanceSport "is highly democratic, accommodating all ages and abilities in appropriate ways, and does not require extra equipment or heavy expenditure for beginners." While, in my opinion, this is not entirely true, this statement does contain solid elements of truth. Though decidedly not the "rule," I have personally experienced instances of implicit "aggression" during competition, like intentionally being "boxed in" ("ungentlemanly behavior"). Similarly, competition does require some equipment (e.g. dance shoes and in most instances instruction and coaching). Keen amateur, competition and DanceSport are more about appearing to be effortlessly dancing two as one, while addressing viewer appeal than "beating" other couples in any way possible.

From an alternative perspective, that of DanceSport performance, Picart argued that dance should project an archetypal emotion (such as romance, passion, or sexual desire) while linking them to a visually produced set of feelings (for example, fear, anxiety, anger). All push usual dance genre boundaries, incorporating, for example, gangs, primitivism, pseudo-striptease and same sex partner dance. I personally think it important not to confuse Hollywood/Broadway style dance "storied" performances and more typical, partnered ballroom performances. In typical partnered ballroom performance, it is more about interpreting music and effortlessly performing various ballroom figures. The "story," if any, may or may not have elements of strong emotion, feelings, or social concerns. More important is whether it presents an overall dance/music visual representation using ballroom and ballroom-based figures to the audience's satisfaction. I am aware, for example, of cadres of dancers, mainly from within the modern dance genre, who consciously and actively explore social issues in dance. Using "excess" to promote dance, however, falls into my category of "movie/stage tricks."

Young Adults

Creating performance and competitive dance routines, particularly the information gathering and decision-making aspects, is a direct example of higher order thinking—one of the most valuable age-appropriate kinds of learning for young adults. In my experience, through dance, young adults can learn discipline, discover their innate talents, become more consciously aware of body feelings, experience inspiration, conquer stress, participate in teamwork, build self-confidence and both recognize and show empathy, acceptance and forgiveness.

Dance has a particularly important effect on physical activity and wellness. This is especially so with partner dancing at all levels of ballroom dance. Ballroom dancing typically requires partners to dance without stopping for up to two and a half minutes. Competitive dance requires the same, then after a quick 10-second break, continuing on to a next dance, often up to five times or more for each dance or combination of dances to reach the finals! Each such dance round has been said to be comparable to five two-minute sprints, which, over time can reap the physical rewards of both a sprinter and a long-distance runner (McCabe).

Ballroom dancing, fortunately, while excellent physical exercise, is also a low-impact activity, building not only cardiovascular reserve, but also muscle strength and tone in the legs, back and arms, resulting in better posture and grace. The hazards related to many typical "gym" exercises don't necessarily apply to ballroom dance. Other benefits include increased flexibility. Joint pain later in life is often the result of tight muscles creating ligament tension affecting the joints. Flexibility in young adulthood has been found to increase the body's resilience to physical stress and help avoid and mitigate immediate and long term injury. But dance isn't just for young adults (McCabe; Liiv; Ballroom Dancing).

In addition to objective studies, Lakes stated "participation in partnered dance styles is associated with perceived improvements in physical fitness, cognitive and social function, mood, and self-confidence, and that perceived benefits may increase as individuals dance more frequently and over longer periods of time."

Children

While there are growing numbers of studies regarding adult ballroom dancers in peer-reviewed medical literature, there are, at this time, considerably fewer about children, causing more reliance on social media articles. Ballroom dance, emphasizing partnered dance, can help children develop emotionally, socially and cognitively. By learning perseverance and self-motivation in partnership dance, children learn to solve problems through cooperative experimentation. It is important that children learn, if they don't succeed, to make mistakes, and ask for help, and accept constructive feedback in order to improve (Malamov; Spirov).

According to Malamov and Spirov, children develop enhanced sensory awareness and explore nonverbal communication, which together represent roughly two-thirds of all communication. By understanding "body" language, they learn how to portray a message using body movement, and how to interpret body movement signals from others. Many forms of partnership dance, including Ballroom and Latin-American, are inherently social. But partnership dance encourages the development of age-appropriate social relationships. Children learn kindness and appreciation in order to move together in synchrony, share energy and power. Partnership dancers quickly learn to work successfully together and to be patient with one another in different settings. In this manner, children learn to observe, listen, take turns leading and following, and cooperate with each another. As a child, dance helped me to learn to express my ideas and feelings through releasing energy within boundaries, taking delight in what I could do.

Adolescent ballroom dancers, in particular, experience improvement in self-awareness, self-management, social awareness, and relationship skills (Baxter).

Moving one's body to music, especially when done athletically, directs the nervous system to release natural endorphins which produce a sensation of well-being. Runners often talk of the "difficult" first twenty minutes followed by the "joy" of continued exercise. This is a "lesson" in life best learned in childhood (Bigelow; Miller).

Interestingly, Ballroom and Latin-American DanceSport instructor Egor Shalvarov offered the following "4 Reasons Why Your Child SHOULD NOT Ballroom Dance:"

First, Ballroom and Latin-American dancing might not really be the best match for an individual child's personality.

Second, organized dance, like any organized sport, can be expensive. While dance initially requires little equipment—mainly good dance shoes—with time, many children and their parents may opt for group or private lessons. Performances and competitions present additional costs, including event fees, costumes, makeup and traveling expenses. Private coaching for higher level competition can be especially costly.

Third, partnership break ups with attendant feelings of sadness and loss, occasionally anger and hatred, may not be in a particular child's best interest, especially at a young age.

Finally, if a child becomes heavily engaged in performance or competitive DanceSport, it can take a toll on school work and attendance, family gatherings, and other important life events. In the end, it is important to continually ask if it's the child who wants to dance, or the parents?

Toddlers

A toddler's life is a lot about observing and then practicing standing and walking. Through dance, toddlers can learn to coordinate and control their muscles, and in the process, develop better spatial awareness. Toddlers who dance are thought to perform better later in life at school. They may also become more used to listening, following directions, practicing, memorizing and thinking creatively (Babies).

Practice, for toddlers, largely translates into play. Better language acquisition, memory, creativity, practice, patience and perseverance all appear related. Irrespective of age, everyone dances. With its myriad mental, physical and emotional benefits, combined with the fact that one can continue to dance long into the later years, it's an activity that arguably every parent should begin with their toddler. But both toddlers and parents are benefactors from rhythmic personal attention, and for toddlers, this is greatly magnified (Kragness; Brown).

Infants

Surprisingly, there is more in the scientific literature about rhythmic mother-infant interaction than dance in toddlers and children. Clearly, the power of dance extends further back then childhood. Infants are born with many pre-programmed reflexes. These reflexes are the bases for eating, reaching, sitting and crawling. Dance movements build on these primitive natural reflexes, especially reaching, crawling and later walking. Rhythmic movements elevate heart rate and activate muscles. Rhythmic movements, especially in synchrony with those of a parent, engage the senses, allowing an infant to experience pleasurable movement and stimulation leading quickly to rolling, pre-walking, bouncing and flying before being able to move independently (Bell).

Not to forget the powerful effect of soothing touch, when a baby is placed into a person's arms, the holder instinctively begin to rock the baby back and forth, especially to any music. Mothers often weave together fascinating movement, song and soothing words that help both participants thrive. When done to music or singing, it exposes the baby to different sounds, tones, chords and rhythms that quickly become associated with different pleasing body sensations and movements. Dancing with one's baby can also be just plain fun. If dancing in front of a mirror or near another dancing parent-infant pair, both members of the partnership often seem to watch the others and mimic their gestures and body movements (Bell; Dissanayake, Hoch).

Pregnancy

Dancing clearly offers benefits to adults, young adults, children, infants, toddlers and babies. But could dancing also be beneficial to mother, fetus and maybe even life partner during pregnancy? The short answer is, done in moderation, very likely yes. While there have been many studies on the effects of *music* on mother and fetus, objective studies on the effects of moderate social and keen amateur partner *dance* on mother, fetus and life partner are few and far between. However, most health care providers would, at the least, acknowledge that exercise is beneficial to the mother to guard against depression, to the fetus in terms of better growth, development and resiliency, and to the father to maintain participatory attention (Sanders).

Current guidelines from The American College of Obstetricians and Gynecologists suggest that mothers who are highly active before a healthy pregnancy should be able to continue high-intensity exercise without adverse affects to mother or fetus. Likewise, the United States Centers for Disease Control and Prevention encourages at least 150 minutes of moderate aerobic "walking" activity each week, pregnant or not. And what is social dance but "glorified walking?" Pregnancy may require that one "take it a littler easier," but not so easy as to skip dancing altogether. Dancing for short periods of time every day is considered by most to be safe if one's doctor gives the go-ahead. If one listens to one's body and adapts non-violent dance routines, e.g. without "lifts," it's unlikely to "overdo" things (Stahl "Physical Activity").

Sherry Moore identified five major prenatal benefits that come from partnered social ballroom dance:

1) Social and keen amateur partner dance help develop and maintain cardiovascular reserve. A weight-resisting activity like dance when danced with "connection," can provide a good "cardio workout." It engages the entire body rather than just isolated muscle groups. Additionally, good dance frame encourages proper posture, though small modifications to the frame may need to be made especially during the last trimester.

2) Partner dance is low impact—ballroom dance is one of the better low-impact forms of exercise available, whether pregnant or not. Furthermore, ballroom dance halls and studios are most often equipped with shock absorbent wood flooring to minimize impact on joints. This is especially important to the body when carrying extra weight.

3) Dance reduces stress and boosts energy levels not only in the mother but also in the dance partner. Both partners can enjoy the social aspects of being together and with others, and dance promotes a restful night's sleep.

4) Social and keen amateur partner ballroom dance can improve muscle tone, flexibility and strength as well as skin tone and elasticity. Dance is an excellent way to build, lengthen, condition and coordinate muscles, while conditioning

nerves and strengthening one's overall physical condition in preparation for childbirth. Prenatal dance should, for safety's sake, begin with warmup and stretching (see .American Pregnancy Association).

5) Finally, partnered ballroom dance is a complex of beneficial aerobic exercises for all ages and stages in life. When committed to, and practiced consistently and safely, one can reap major health benefits that fall far beyond the immediate improvements in physical endurance, weight management and agility. Additional benefits often include decreased blood pressure, lower cholesterol and improvement in cardiovascular health. To these, add increased lung capacity, decreased bone loss, improved balance with lower risk of falls, better posture, reduced risk of anxiety and depression, reduced risk of developing type-two diabetes. After pregnancy also add improved socialization, and reduced expression of degenerative cognitive diseases in later life like dementia and possibly Alzheimer's.

Seniors

In the USA, USA Dance's DanceSport Rule Book. defined a competitive "senior DanceSport Athlete couple" as a partnership in which one partner "must have reached their 35th birthday or more in the calendar year and the other partner must have reached his or her 30th birthday or more in the calendar year." Seniors are further broken down into five subcategories ending in Senior V defined as a partnership in which one partner "must have reached their 75th birthday or more in the calendar year and the other partner must have reached his or her 70th birthday or more in the calendar year."

NDCA (National Dance Council of America) similarly defined "senior" competition but presently has no Senior V category.

While in essence, a "senior" in an appropriate partnership can generally be said to be anyone over 35 years, the United States Social Security Administration generally currently defines "senior" as "anyone of retirement age, or a person that has reached age 62 or older. However the standard threshold for Medicaid is age 65." This roughly relates to Senior IV, which, for purposes of this book will be assumed to be "senior" or "elderly."

The benefits of dancing for seniors and elderly are many and varied. The first priority, however, must always be to *prevent* physical accidents, injuries and physical retreat due to aging.

When I coordinated Japanese competitors at Hawaii Star Ball in Honolulu, Hawaii, I would estimate that about 50% were "seniors," with most un-partnered amateur competitors competing "Pro-Am" (professional-amateur). Irrespective of country or origin, senior competitors stretched,, carefully applied stage make up, wore elegant outfits, and made a point of smiling. Even when nervous, they looked young and happy. On the other hand, they'd typically taken a lot of lessons and coaching, and had hours of practice by the time they hit the competition floor. Afterwards, they made it a point to socialize, appearing happy and satisfied, even if the results were not as good as they hoped. I found myself thinking, What makes these people appear so youthful and happy? My opinion is that it is because they are doing what they truly love to do and can afford. Like everyone, competitive dancers don't get younger, they grow older everyday. And, I found myself thinking again, What makes these people appear so young and healthy?

Less than a decade ago, there was little in the scientific/academic literature about dance and health, especially regarding seniors. Nowadays, the United States National Institute of Medicine's PubMed.gov has numerous articles on dance as a physical exercise and sport. This has been my primary source for information on the effects of dance in seniors; an excellent starting point, in my opinion is Keogh's article entitled "Physical benefits of dancing for healthy older adults: a review."

One commonly mentioned benefit of senior dance is preserving, if not improving, bone density and joint health. Dancing is an excellent weight-resisting activity both in terms of movement and frame. Sherry Moore, cited earlier, adds that dancing additionally helps seniors maintain flexible muscle strength and tone, which persists and makes a person more youthful in action and appearance.

As we become older, falls and their consequences become more important. When I was forced to decrease my dancing during the COVID-19 pandemic, I began walking in the morning and evening, alternating dancing at home and resistance exercising every other day. One day, to my surprise, I fell, hitting and scraping my knee. I looked around to see if anyone had seen me fall. Nobody! Even my husband who was walking just ahead of me! Fortunately, I didn't break any bones, tear any muscles or sprain any ligaments. Thank you, Dance! At that time, I realized how dancing engages the whole body and in doing so, optimizes balance and recovery, important for everybody, but especially older people. My partner, a retired physician, says if we don't practice for three weeks, we begin deconditioning, ultimately losing muscle strength and memory. "Use it or lose it!" he likes to say.

According to the United States Centers for Disease Control and Prevention (CDC), adult-onset dementias can cause variable loss of memory often to the point of affecting activities of daily living. The CDC estimates that in 2014, of people at least 65 years of age (corresponding to the senior IV dance competition age group), an estimated five million suffer from some degree of dementia (Minorities and Women Are at Greater Risk for Alzheimer's Disease). It would be interesting to do a lifetime study on partnership ballroom dancers to see if the results are the same.

Do people actually "loose memories?" My partner, not only a retired physician but also a neurobiologist says, "Not usually." Instead, "memory loss" is more about it becoming increasingly difficult to retrieve the memories. If that's true—and I believe it is—then helping to prevent memory decline, at least in dancers, may be a consequence of constantly renewing routines as well as maintaining old and making new social associations, something we do frequently when we socialize and partner dance. Still, there's no escaping it: Cognitive function in many will decline with age. But it's not all bad news. An important key to slowing decline may lie in exercising not only the brain, but the body and brain together.

Adult brains are said to contain stem cells capable of making new brain cells, a process called "neurogenesis." As the brain ages, these stem cells slowly lose their ability to produce new neurons, supposedly causing cognitive function to slowly decline. Bartlett and research colleague, Dr. Blackmore, recently identified that exercise increases production of new brain cells and can improve learning and memory (Queensland Brain Institute "Can you grow new brain cells?").

These two are now heading up a clinical trial monitoring 300 people aged 65 and older to identify the optimal amount, intensity and type of exercise for cognitive *improvement* in the aging brain. "This will be the most comprehensive analysis yet of why exercise is beneficial," Prof Bartlett explains. "Ultimately, we would hope to have clear public health guidelines as to how exercise can both prevent and reverse dementia." Will dance be one of these exercise regimes? I think and hope so (The University of Queensland; Queensland Brain Institute "Memory and Age").

"Dementia...occurs when abnormal proteins accumulate

inside and around neurons. A key to slowing decline may lie in exercising not only the brain, but at the same time the body (Queensland Brain Institute "Memory and Age"). Aging is stressful. The "Golden Years" may be golden, but only for those with youthful bodies and brains. It's more correct, I think, to say that "Youth is wasted on the young." As we age, we begin to think more about health, finances, family, and spouse, easily resulting in anxiety. Even for those who try to be positive, age often makes it more difficult to change one's mood. Dance affords an opportunity to listen to music, move in synchrony and let the body set the mood. What is that? It's eurythmic dancing!

It's nice to be the best at what one does, and dancing is no exception. But there's more to dance than being the best, receiving the loudest applause or winning the biggest trophy. It has been my experience that seniors often change their attitude from winning in competition to that of safely and satisfyingly competing or even just finishing a dance and feeling good about it. It's more about a sense of personal accomplishment or self-actualization. Or call all it "spirituality;" that's how I regard it. What does it feel like? Many dancers, young or old, eventually attain a place where the dance becomes more than moving the body through time and space. It's even more than passion. It's a way of connecting to something greater than oneself and reveling in the assurance that one is part of something greater and never alone.

In summary, dance, especially partnered ballroom dance,

social, performance or competition provides strong benefits throughout one's life from fetus to senior. That's the real power of dance. Great dancing is all about stretching, bending, extending and moving with graceful passion. We go to dance parties, dress up, and make up like a star. It's like being in a movie or acting on stage. It's never too late to dance, whether that means joining a dance circle, taking Ballroom or Latin dance lessons, performing, competing or attending social dance parties. My partner and I say, "It's now or never, so make it now!"

The Power of Dance

Chapter 9
Partnered Ballroom Dance

In this book, I have focused first on ballroom dance, meaning Smooth/Ballroom and Rhythm,/Latin-American dances. Using the generic term "ballroom," I mean partnered Smooth/Ballroom and Rhythm/Latin-American dancing by at least one couple on a ballroom floor.

Most ballroom dancers begin their journey as amateurs. Beginners typically acquire instruction in the fundamentals of ballroom dance through the study of music and figures unique to each of the "classic" partnered ballroom dances. These include Waltz, Quickstep, Foxtrot/Slow Fox, Tango, Viennese Waltz, and Rumba, Cha Cha Cha, Samba, Jive and Paso Doble in the International style; or Waltz, Foxtrot, Tango, Viennese Waltz, and Bolero, Rumba, Cha Cha, Mambo and East Coast Swing in the American Style (USA Dance "Competitor Guide").

Unlike many dances, adding interpretive expression to the above typically involves working with a multi-talented professional teacher and later coach, rather than a choreographic specialist. Group classes typically work best for social dancers, while keen amateurs, performance and competitive couples interested in detail typically benefit more from one-on-one private lessons. DanceSport athletes, as well as future professional dancers who wish to develop advanced material or become future ballroom teachers will often seek coaching. At its highest level, partnered ballroom dance, or DanceSport, is said to be both a performing and competitive athletic *sport*.

There are significant differences between ballroom and modern, jazz, ballet and stage dance. The ballroom dances, for example, typically express and explore male-female (or at least partnership) roles and relationships. Second, social and competitive ballroom dancers choose the musical genre (though not the particular musical piece) to which they will dance. Finally, it is common in modern, jazz, ballet or staged dance, but not necessarily ballroom dance, for the creative process to be developed by a professional choreographer. Like a movie producer, the choreographer typically chooses the music, figures and dancers. Again, like a movie director, he or she weaves everything together into a coherent composition. In short, the product is built to progressively approach what the *choreographer* envisions as the final product.

DanceSport routines, on the other hand, typically evolve from the figures which a couple does best together. Dancers and coach amalgamate these figures using expressive figures and movements called "techniques." Unlike performance, during actual competition, all these elements are not fully under competitor or coach control. In social dance, they are moderately constrained, but couples are free to otherwise interpret, adding relaxed "fun" and "enjoyment" to the activity.

Social and Keen Amateur Dance

All types of ballroom dance, including DanceSport, generally begin with dancers exploring their own native movements and qualities. Unlike modern, jazz, ballet and staged dance, social ballroom dance is built almost exclusively on "natural walking movements," and is danced for the couple's enjoyment and delight.

Emmanuel said that the special quality of classical Greek dance is that sometimes lacking in precision, it displays perfect rhythm—not a bad definition of social dance. According to Emmanuel, ancient Greek dancers often danced to celebrate memorable moments of their lives, whether a battle, funeral, sexual encounter or any other event through dance. Likewise, social ballroom dances often, but not always have a theme.

Chace said that dance reawakens "kinesthetic sense," allowing body and mind to be developed and, where possible, healed. Said another way, through partnered ballroom dance, people can rediscover and reawaken parts of their bodies that are not normally felt, do not move or are not readily mentally available. Dance, however, involves "something more." It involves relearning to move, and by connecting movements with the felt or kinesthetic sense of movement, more "authentically" communicating, self-actualizing and healing.

Social ballroom dance activities tend to promote health

and healing, and can bind people together where distance and time tend to separate them. Addressing distance, social ballroom dance has evolved into two basic "styles:" International and American. Both share most ballroom dances (though their techniques may differ), while, at the same time, they both include a few dances unique to the style. Time is the other factor that separates. Consider, for example, a recent comment by a visiting dancer after three years of no public dances due to COVID: "Does anyone still dance International-style in Hawaii?" In addition, each nation and era has its own dances, clothing and manners of expression. Reynolds reminded that social partner dance events have begun exploring a change from two styles to one "World" dance style, and ultimately One-World DanceSport in anticipation of Olympic DanceSport.

With social ballroom dance, it's all about how one feels. The ultimate goal of social ballroom dancing is, after all, self-enjoyment. At the next level, keen amateur ballroom dance usually begins with observing natural body movements in mirrors while walking (Standard) or moving hip and torso (Latin-American) to better express and participate in a particular musical genre. Modern, jazz, ballet and stage dancers do not commonly perform or compete in specialized male-female partnerships using close, closed hold frame. For this reason alone, ballroom figures, movements, routines, choreography and notation differ considerably from their analogs in modern dance. With keen amateur dance, it's all about self-satisfaction and the quality of dance.

Some social dancers will study the standardized figures (syllabi) with or without professional instruction. Keen amateurs, often called "advanced" or "pre-championship" level dancers by the World DanceSport Federation are not bound by ISTD's *The Ballroom Technique* or *The Revised Technique* (World DanceSport Federation "rules" and "syllabus").

Everyone dances. If there are 7.5 billion people in the world today, at least 7 billion are likely dancers whether they know it or not.

In America, there would eventually emerge one set of syllabi for social dancers and another "stricter" set for "keen amateurs." While USA studios were developing primarily these two levels, ISTD in the meantime was busy reassembling international syllabi into student, associate, and member/fellow teacher proficiency levels.

Keen amateurs with professional teaching and practice have become outstanding performance or competitive dancers, dancing for both personal and public pleasure.

Performance Dance

Partnered performance ballroom dance is all about choreography and outstanding execution. These days, however, it's no longer necessarily a question about how well one dances the named figures listed in ISTD's *The Ballroom Technique* or *The Revised Technique*. In my experience, it's about a stunning opener, the most impressive dance routine one can muster, and a spectacular ending. In fact, stunning openings and spectacular endings typically don't utilize standard named figures, but rather interesting amalgamations of advanced or unnamed figures like in Moore's *Popular Variations*. From the moment a couple commits to performance ballroom dance, "the sky's the limit" as long as it leaves the audience with "chickenskin." In fact, the way my partner and I evaluate our performances is by seeking afterwards to discover if the audience as well as us, experienced chickenskin during our performance, and if so, when exactly.

Ellen Jacob, in *Dancing—A Guide for the Dancer You Can Be*, pointed out that in modern, jazz and stage dance, a professional choreographer usually acts as the "designer" of the dance. In ballroom performance dance, the choreographer is commonly a professional, typically one's dance instructor or competition coach. The highest level DanceSport competitors almost exclusively utilize a professional choreographer. Jacob states that DanceSport choreographers commonly work holistically with a competitive couple to highlight their strengths and in the long-term strengthen their weaknesses.

Merriam-Webster's *Collegiate Dictionary* defines choreography as the art of representing dance symbolically with a focus on composition and arrangement of dance figures. The attraction of today's DanceSport comes not so much from dancing precisely pre-scripted routines, but rather from two people, traditionally, but not necessarily exclusively a male and female, dancing as one. Most choreographed works are recorded using a standard notation system, often with individual embellishments. Ballroom and Latin-American performances are often precursors to competition and DanceSport, which almost always use carefully pre-scripted choreography. In performance ballroom dance, the emphasis shifts from personal enjoyment and satisfaction. It's all about what viewers see and feel rather than what the dancer does, feels or thinks.

Performance ballroom dance typically starts with each partner asking several creative process questions: Do you enjoy sustained, smooth-flowing motions or sharp, abrupt motions? Are your movements heavy and forceful or light and delicate? Do you feel rooted to the ground or like you are flying through space and time? Do you seem to make broad, sweeping gestures or move on a smaller, more contained scale? Are you suddenly doing tic movements with complex rhythms or sticking to simple rhythms, shapes and figures? Which body parts do you isolate and which muscle groups seem to move naturally to music?

Unlike social, keen amateur and competitive dance where selection of the music is often outside the dancers' control, performance dance allows one to select the "perfect" music for the couple. The "best" performance music is, in my opinion, something with which the audience can identify, that is dramatic or powerful in nature, and plays directly to the dancers' strengths.

It seems natural to assume that creative processes, in ballet, modern and jazz dance as well as ballroom performance dance would be much the same. Unfortunately, just as the definition of choreography depends to some extent on the form, kind, and level of dance and dancers, so do the creative processes involved.

Maurice Emmanuel, a Doctor of Arts and Doctor Laureate of the Paris Conservatory of Dance, explained in his book, *The Antique Greek Dance*, to ancient Greeks, dance was inseparable from music. Music was a gift of the Muses (inspiration). It blends combinations of tones into a whole that has timing, rhythm, melody, harmony, structure and continuity.

According to Clarke and Crisp, dance and music share and mutually enhance two key attributes, namely rhythm and structure, to which I would add timing, since timing technically is different from but just as essential as rhythm. At its simplest, dance is a bodily expression of music.

One huge difference between social/keen amateur dance and performance dance is that performance dance is typically performed "live." It may be recorded and re-shown digitally, but the initial performance is typically before a live audience.

"Since movement is essential for survival, our brains are highly stimulated by watching people dance—their motions, body language, facial expressions and gestures pull us in. And according to the mirror system theory, we can vicariously feel a dancer's movement in our own bodies" (Stahl "We're Born to Love Dance").

Competition Dance (including DanceSport)

Competition ballroom dance is quite different from social and performance ballroom dance. But first, it's important to define what, exactly "competition" ballroom dance is. You'd think that with all the different ballroom organizations and competitions, there would be a single, common definition. There isn't. In fact, most ballroom competition organizations write a lot about the details, but rarely actually define what ballroom or competition is.

Jonathan Enrique, a certified ballroom dance teacher for Ballroom Dance Planet, in a blog article entitled "What is Dancesport Competitive Ballroom Dancing?" stated, "DanceSport competitive ballroom dancing is a competition where couples on a dance floor are compared to others by the most qualified judges." This statement implies what is often commonly assumed: that competitive ballroom dancing and DanceSport are one and the same. However, they aren't, though through advertising and television they are increasingly *assumed* to be one and the same. It is important therefore to make a further distinction between competition ballroom dancing and DanceSport.

In my experience, competitive ballroom dancing occurs whenever two or more ballroom dance couples agree to dance on a dance floor and be ranked by qualified judges in front of an audience. The fact that the event is generally "live" and in front of an audience is what performance and competitive ballroom dance share. In fact, even this definition has its limitations, as, according to the USA Dance's "Competitor

Guide," competition ballroom dance includes three events—Pro-Am, Show Dance and Cabaret—which though partnered, can be competed or judged "solo" on the dance floor like a performance or be judged and ranked within proficiency and age categories.

Technically, DanceSport in the USA "takes place under the Rules of USA Dance, DanceSport Division and the Dance Sport Council. USA Dance is the member body of the WDSF (USA Dance "Competitor Guide"), and includes International and America-style dance as well as International 10-Dance, American 9-Dance, Theatrical Ballroom, Show Dance and Cabaret. In addition, some competitions will add additional dance events, or hold a team match (where multiple couples each dance one dance and the winning team is based on the combined score of all couples on each team) or a "Jack and Jill" competition (USA Dance "Competitor Guide"). World DanceSport competitions are currently held under the rules and auspices of the WDSF or its affiliates, which have the power to amend or interpret these rules. Other competitive ballroom dance organizations include the National Dance Council of America (NDCA), World Dance Organization (WDO) and a plethora of new organizations, each establishing their own competition ballroom or DanceSport rules.

Ballroom dance competitions and DanceSport currently use a "skating system" introduced by the British Official Board of Ballroom Dancing (now British Dance Council) in 1937 to determine competitive rank. It has two major levels.

The first level applies to preliminary rounds up to and including the semifinals. The second level applies to the final round. In all but the final round, progressing to the next round depends on the number of "pass" marks received. In the final round, ranking is determined by a complex system involving assignment of the majority of judges of a particular rank. There are 10 "final round" rules that can be applied to adjust the final rankings and tie-break. This skating system is used because there are usually multiple couples on the floor that can be observed, each for only a very short time.

As stated above, ballroom dance competition as well as DanceSport couples generally compete against each other before an audience and are judged using the Skating System: Those couples that attract attention while executing a particular figure or movement which they are particularly good at score higher. It is not as important to command constant attention and dance a perfect, cohesive dance. It is more important to constantly convey the impression of effortless dancing, while inviting the attention of judges and audience at key "highlight" moments that show the partnership at its best.

Whether under the rubric "competitive ballroom dance" or "DanceSport," competition partners constantly observe each other both separately and together to answer the basic question: What do we, as a couple, naturally do best together? After every practice dance for a competition, my partner and I discuss what we did best together and how it will look to judges and audience.

As such, routines in DanceSport commonly consist of dance phrases that demonstrate basic (sometimes called "compulsory," though in "open" competition they are not strictly compulsory) figures. These are interspersed with unexpected, quick, unusual movements called variations or "tricks." These are important to break stride, rhythm, or even create photographic opportunities. The objective in DanceSport is not to be consistent in all parts of a dance routine. What is more important is interweaving the expected with the unexpected in a unique way. This should focus attention on partnership abilities at opportune moments and is a major coaching goal. Hence, the importance of choreography in competitive ballroom dance and DanceSport as in performance ballroom dance, all of which are nonetheless different and in some way(s) unique.

Competitors typically compete at different proficiency as well as age levels. Proficiency Levels include Syllabus (fixed dance figures in Bronze, Silver, Gold) and Open Levels (no fixed figures at the Novice, Pre-Championship and Championship Levels). Each Level emphasizes basic classes of body movements. For example, the International-style ballroom dances (Waltz, Foxtrot, Tango, Quickstep and Viennese Waltz) involve not just individual figures and movements but also "two moving as one." The International-style Latin-American dances, (Rumba, Cha Cha Cha, Samba, Jive and Paso Doble) involve demonstrating the movement of energy from one partner to the other and back (especially with "gooey" connection mentioned earlier) enlisting every muscle to express feelings through strong lead and follow (USA Dance "Competitor Guide").

The Power of Dance

Chapter 10
The Future

So far, I've focused on what currently is, in regard to the power of partner ballroom dance. I'd now like to take a moment to consider what might yet be—the future of partnered ballroom dance: its potential and where it's going.

My focus has on the power of partner dance from a distinctly "Western" point-of-view. According to World Population Review:

> The most widely accepted modern definition of the 'Western World' is based...upon the cultural (or when appropriate, political or economic) identities of the countries in question. Using this definition, the Western World includes Europe as well as any countries whose cultures are strongly influenced by European values or whose populations include many people descended from European colonists—for example Australia, New Zealand, and most countries in North and South America. ("Western Countries 2022")

But Western Culture applies to only a limited percentage of the world by population or land mass as well as purportedly World Partner Dance.

According to Western mythology, of the nine Muses (*Mousai* or inspirations), all of whom enjoyed dancing, Terpsichore was the preeminent goddess of dance. In fact, her name, translated, means "Delighting in Dance" ("TERPSIKHORE"). However, non-Western cultures throughout the world over time have had many named gods and goddesses of dance. For example, I'm Japanese, and, in Japanese mythology, the Shinto goddess Ame-no-Uzume is known as a master of merry-making, humor and dance (Wright).

While partnered ballroom dancing remains primarily "Western" in terms of its conception and application, many world cultures have their own god(dess)es, icons and styles of partner dance, often beginning in pre-mythology and religion. I foresee a plausible future world where the spirituality inherent within these early dances becomes more universally acknowledged. That is to say, a future where partnered ballroom dance as well as its newest competitive form, DanceSport, speak increasingly to spiritually. In today's world of religious conflict, dance promotes individual spiritual health, growth and knowledge through exploration of music and rhythms. As such, humans can come to recognize and even delight in shared spirituality through dance with others. NOTE: I make here a distinction between *spirituality* and the human "business of spirituality" called *religion*.

I have maintained my focus throughout this work tightly on partnered dance, and for a reason: Partnership in ballroom dance, whether social, performance or competition, is a singularly important aspect of the power of dance. Partner dance grounds the dancers in terms of humanism, cooperation, friendship, teamwork, respect, empathy and compromise.

The mere existence of other non-Western points-of-view suggests that partnered ballroom dance presents the opportunity of partnered ballroom dance growing well beyond Western cultural assumptions and limitations. To some extent this has already begun. As the WDSF admits more and more organizations into its group of DanceSport certifying bodies (e.g. USA Dance for USA), different cultural considerations will undoubtably begin surfacing and have to be addressed. One plausible approach is, of course, "World" Olympic DanceSport.

DanceSport is sometimes said to be the epitome of partnered ballroom dance, and seems in fact, to have evolved specifically to open the door to World Olympic Dance as a sport. However, there remain several outstanding "roadblocks:"

First, current DanceSport is, as mentioned above, traditionally "Western" in its cultural underpinnings.

Second, while competitive ballroom dance and DanceSport use the "skating system" in competition, the World Olympics use what might best be described as a tripartite system. For similar sports (1) nations rank their athletes by national standards for eligibility; (2) Olympic events use a points-accumulated placement system, and (3) athletes and nations are ranked on a medal accumulation strategy (International Olympic Committee. "Olympic Charter").

Third, most Olympic events concern individual or team sports. Partnered sports like ice dancing are rare, and considered by some to be an "exception to the rule."

Fourth, in 2020, the Year of the COVID-19 Pandemic, the IOC announced that breakdancing would debut in the 2024 Paris Olympic Games. It is a popular, well-monied, single person activity appealing directly to youth and quite amenable to Olympic-style scoring. With the temporary cessation of most partnered ballroom dancing as well as DanceSport competition before live audiences, it was hoped that breakdancing might continue to keep open the door to DanceSport in future Olympics. Breakdancing, however, carries with it an additional barrier to partnered DanceSport becoming an Olympic event: Breaking (or breakdancing) is non-partnered. How this will ultimately effect partnered ballroom dancing's claim as a future Olympic sport is not known.

Fifth, there remains the question whether DanceSport is, in fact, a sport.

Finally, most Olympic events are male or female, but not male-female-coupled.

Nonetheless, I believe it is time for partnered ballroom dance and its competitive reflection, DanceSport, to become an Olympic sporting event, and continue to wait patiently for it to happen. A lot of people social dance. Even in a wheelchair, partners can dance. Partner dance, whether based on male-female participation or more correctly, lead and follow, is a performing art requiring and displaying what I consider to be an expression of the highest level of athletic as well as technical skill. That is to say, a sport.

Lifelong Devotion

After learning ballroom dancing, I found word "Dance therapy" an article in Dance View, a popular Japanese dance magazine (I am Japanese after all). I explored Dance Movement Therapy (DMT), until I realized that it was heavily weighted towards Sigmund Freud's psychology of the mind, rather than Wilhelm Reich's somatic approach, more amenable in terms of dance. Furthermore, DMT seemed more attuned to individual "modern dance" rather than partnership dance. Why was this, I wondered, given the unique power of partnered ballroom dance? What came to me was that (1) partnered ballroom dance is basically a non-language-driven somatic experience where "the mind follows the body." whereas DMT seemed basically an offshoot of "talk therapy" driven by controlled somatic experiences where "the body follows the mind."

Partner ballroom dance, with its strong social aspect and two-dancing-as-one emphasis, proved to me a challenging variation on DMT. What I eventually settled on was "somatic therapy," with an emphasis on two-people-dancing/breathing-as-one in their dance and the accompanying music, creating a shared, non-language-dependent experience expressed through partnered dance itself.

The power of partner dance is present throughout one's lifetime. As one gets older, the body naturally ages. These days, I am sometimes concerned about my body when dancing, as it is more challenging to move as smoothly and naturally through time and space as I want. I find myself stretching more often and with more difficulty in order to maintain my dance flexibility. It is my lifelong devotion to dance that, I believe, in the end, especially benefits me at this time of life with the power of dance. For the rest of my life, as long as I possibly can, I plan to walk, stretch my body and dance with my partner.

Devoting oneself to partner dance, means always trying to cultivate a common or at least a shared visual inner feeling and emotion. It is from these shared inner feelings that the spiritually transcendent nature of dance emerges. This is the greatest expression of the power of dance.

One phenomenon that inspired me in my lifelong devotion to partnered ballroom dancing was the inclusion of partnered dance "in the movies." Cinematic performances are unlike social, performance or competition. They are a category unique unto themselves with the opportunity to take and retake dance phrases over and over until visually perfect, with the added drama of carefully selected music, lighting and camera angles. In addition, true commercial cinematic performance dance includes a chance at "immortality." I can say this with authority, having now appeared in several films. While a complex and often frustrating venue, there is, quite simply, nothing like seeing oneself dance on the silver screen.

In conclusion, life often creates setbacks, but there is something in partnership ballroom dance that will always be part of my and my partner's lives together. Everyone, young or old, moves their body through time and space. Though the "moves" may be different, everyone dances. The power of dance is that while everyone dances through life, partnered ballroom in particular encourages the healthiest, fullest, most robust and rich life possible. Perhaps it's time now to stop reading and thinking about partner ballroom dance and just do it!

WORKS CITED

"1939 Ballroom Dancing 4th Edition by Alex Moore," The Ballroom Dance Encyclopedia, no date, http://dancepedia.info/top/library/instruction-manual/ballroom-dancing-by-alex-moore/. Accessed 30 Jul 2021.

2002 USA DanceSport Rules "DANCESPORT RULES, BYLAWS & POLICIES" https://usadance.org/page/DanceSportRules. Accessed 13 June 2022.

Adler, Bill. Fred Astaire: A Wonderful Life. New York, Carroll & Graf Publishers, 1987.

American Dance Therapy Association. No Date. "What is Dance/Movement Therapy?" https://adta.memberclicks.net/what-is-dancemovement-therapy. Accessed 29 June 2022.

American International Dance Association (AIDA). "American Syllabi Step List & Tempi." 2021. https://usistd.org/syllabi-technique/american-style/. Accessed 5 November 2021.

American Pregnancy Association. "16 Ways to Bond With Your Baby While Pregnant." 2021. https://americanpregnancy.org/healthy-pregnancy/while-pregnant/16-ways-to-bond-with-your-baby-while-pregnant/. Accessed 8 July 2022.
---. "Effects of Exercise During Pregnancy." 2021. https://americanpregnancy.org/healthy-pregnancy/is-it-safe/exercise-during-pregnancy-2/. Accessed 8 July 2022.

"Babies are born to dance, new research shows." 16 March 2010. https://www.sciencedaily.com/releases/2010/03/100315161925.htm. Accessed 7 July 2022.

"Ballroom dance." 4 February 2022. https://en.wikipedia.org/wiki/Ballroom_dance. Accessed 26 February 2022.

Ballroom Dancing for Improved Flexibility. 1 Apr 2014. Elite Dance Studio. https://www.elitedancestudio.net/blogs/ballroom-dancing-for-improved-flexibility/. Accessed 6 July 2022.

Baxter, Ashley. "Participation in Ballroom Dancing: The effects on the social and emotional intelligence of adolescents." 1 December 2020. https://digscholarship.unco.edu/cgi/viewcontent.cgi?article=1238&context=theses. Accessed 6 July 2022.

Bell, Martha Ann. "Mother-child behavioral and physiological synchrony." 27 January 2020. Adv Child Dev Behav. 2020;58:163-188

Bigelow, Lisa. "Does Dancing Release Endorphins?" No Date. https://healthyliving.azcentral.com/dancing-release-endorphins-5764.html. Accessed 6 July 2022.

"Bolero." 2021. https://www.music4dance.net/dances/bolero. Accessed 29 November 2021.

Bonner, Shaw and Worthen-Chaudhari, Lise. "The Demographics of Dance in the United States." Journal of dance medicine & science January 1999.

Bose, Swapnil Dhruv. "Alfred Hitchcock reveals the secret ingredient for creating suspense." 8 July 2020. https://faroutmagazine.co.uk/alfred-hitchcock-reveals-secret-to-creating-suspense/. Accessed 19 February 2022.

"Boston (dance)." 2019. https://en.wikipedia.org/wiki/Boston_(dance). Accessed 17 November 2021.

Bowery Waltz. Filmed by Thomas A. Edison. Performers unknown. 1897. https://www.youtube.com/watch?v=UcTYL2L2kQ0. Accessed 19 November 2021.

Brady, Bradford and Maron, John. "On the Record: What was first song on TV show 'American Bandstand'?" 11 October 2020. https://heraldcourier.com/community/on-the-record-what-was-first-song-on-tv-show-american-bandstand/article_5fa5f546-be51-5a3e-b862-365cbdeb3428.html. Accessed 6 December 2021.

Brown, Stephanie. "Exploring Movement With Toddlers and Dance/" 4 June 2020. https://www.verywellfamily.com/toddlers-and-dance-289704. Accessed 7 July 2022.

Castle, Vernon and Castle, Irene. Modern Dancing. New York. Harper & Brothers 1914.

Chaiklin, Sharon and Schmais, Claire. "The Chace Approach to Dance Therapy" in Sandel, Susan, Chaiklin, Sharon and Lohn, Ann (Eds) Foundations of Dance/Movement Therapy: The Life and Work of Marian Chace. Columbia, Marian Chace Memorial Fund and the American Dance Therapy Association 1993.

Chick Webb with Ella Fitzgerald - Rock It For Me [1937]. 21 September 2020. https://www.youtube.com/watch?v=pkXhfoEZanw. Accessed 6 December 2021.

Clarke, Mary and Crisp, Clement. The History of Dance. New York, Crown Publishers Inc., 1981.

"Competitor Guide." No Date. https://usadance.org/page/Competitor-Guide. Accessed 26 February 2022.

Comte, Natalie. Europe, 1450 to 1789: Encyclopedia of the Early Modern World Vol. 2. New York: Charles Scribner's Sons, 2004.

Crozier, Gladys. Beattie. The Tango and how to dance it. London, Andrew Melrose, 1913.

Dance Vision. "Vintage DVDs." 2021. https://shop.dancevision.com/collections/vintage-dvds. Accessed 5Aug 2021.

Deasy, Kristin. "A Brief Introduction to Milonga, Tango's Quick-Footed Cousin." 22 May 2018. https://theculturetrip.com/south-america/argentina/articles/a-brief-introduction-to-milonga-tangos-quick-footed-cousin/. Accessed 21 November 2021.

"Dirty Dancing." First Season/First Episode written by Eleanor Bergstein, Benjamin J. Frost and Brian Volk-Weiss, directed by Brian Volk-Weiss, The Nacelle Company, 2019-2020.

Dirty Dancing - 2. "Mambo". 8 Oct 2009. https://www.youtube.com/watch?v=lkqA_jj4Flk. Accessed 3 December 2021.

Dissanayake, Ellen. "Ancestral human mother-infant interaction was an adaptation that gave rise to music and dance." 30 September 2021. Behav Brain Sci. 2021 Sep 30;44:e68.

Dodworth, Allen. Dancing and its relations to education and social life with a new method of instruction, including a complete guide to the cotillion (German) with 250 figures. From the Library of Congress. https://www.loc.gov/resource/musdi.186.0?st=pdf&pdfPage=1. Accessed 29 May 2022.

Eddie Torres and His Mambo Kings Orchestra and All Star Dancers. Directed by Mitch Frohman. 27 May 2011. https://www.youtube.com/watch?v=jOtWmGhWp1g. Accessed 3 December 2021.

"Elvis Presley - That's All Right (Audio)." 22 July 2015. https://www.youtube.com/watch?v=DCP_g7X31nI. Accessed 6 December 2021.

Emmanuel, Maurice. The Antique Greek Dance. Binsted Hampshire, Noverre press 2012.

Enge, Nick. "Foxtrot." 2019. Library of Dance. https://www.libraryof-dance.org/dances/fox-trot/. Accessed 25 July 2022.

Engel, Lyle Kenyon (Ed). The Fred Astaire Dance Book. New York, Cornerstone Library, 1962.

Fells, Geoffrey. "History of PasoDoble" in Dance Forums. 5 January 2010. https://www.dance-forums.com/threads/history-of-pasodoble.35111/. Accessed 26 September 2021.

Flying Down to Rio [1933]. Directed by Thornton Freeland. Starring Dolores del Río, Ginger Rogers and Fred Astaire. 10 Dec 2012. "Carioca" clip (3 minutes 51 seconds). https://www.youtube.com/watch?v=l8iw69RExbk. Accessed 10 June 2022.

Garber, James J. Harmony in Healing: The Theoretical Basis of Ancient and Medieval Medicine. New York, Rutledge, 2017

Gleissner, Greta. "What Is Dance Movement Therapy?" 12 April 2017. https://www.psychologytoday.com/us/blog/hope-eating-disorder-recovery/201704/what-is-dance-movement-therapy. Accessed 29 June 2022.

Godel, Sarah. "Ballroom: The Dance That Globalization Built." 2012. https://sophia.smith.edu/blog/danceglobalization/2012/05/02/ball-room-the-dance-that-globalization-built-2/. Accessed 3 July 2022.

Gorman, Tom. "Lawrence Welk, a bandleader for millions, dies." 19 May 1992. https://www.baltimoresun.com/news/bs-xpm-1992-05-19-1992140214-story.html. Accessed 4 December 2021.

Guest, Ann Hutchinson. Choreo-Graphics - A Comparison of Dance Notation Systems From the Fifteenth Century to the Present. Amsterdam, Gordon and Breach, 1998.

----, Labanotation: The System of Analyzing and Recording Movement. New York, Routledge 2005.

Hoch, Justine E. "'Dancing' Together: Infant-Mother Locomotor Synchrony." Child Dev. 2021 Jul;92(4):1337-1353.

Herbison-Evans, Dan. "Eight Great Minutes." Dancing USA. Jan/Feb 2002:42.

Howard, Guy. Technique of Ballroom Dancing. Brighton, International Dance Publications, 1995

"How break dancing made the leap from 80s pop culture to the Olympic stage." 9 February 2021. https://usadance.org/news/551409/How-break-dancing-made-the-leap-from-80s-pop-culture-to-the-Olympic-stage.htm. Accessed 14 Nov 2021.

Indie Film Hustle. "6 Filmmaking Techniques Alfred Hitchcock Used To Create Suspense." 14 June 2021. https://indiefilmhustle.com/hitchcock-create-suspense/. Accessed 19 February 2022.

In Gay Madrid. A film by Robert Z. Leonard. 17 May 1930. https://www.youtube.com/watch?v=CNWWj29sjME. Accessed 8 June 2022.

International Olympic Committee. "Olympic Charter." 2021. https://stillmed.olympics.com/media/Document%20Library/OlympicOrg/General/EN-Olympic-Charter.pdf. Accessed 19 August 2022.

ISTD (The Imperial Society of Teachers of Dancing). "Discover Our History." No Date, https://www.istd.org/discover/our-history/. Accessed 10 September 2021.

---. "Discover Our Mission." No Date. https://www.istd.org/discover/our-mission/. Accessed 6 June 2022.

---. The Ballroom Technique. London, The Imperial Society of Teachers of Dancing, 1994.

---. The Ballroom Technique. London, The Imperial Society of Teachers of Dancing, 1986.

---. The Ballroom Technique. London, The Imperial Society of Teachers of Dancing, 1948.

---. The Ballroom Technique. London, The Imperial Society of Teachers of Dancing, 1936.

---. The Revised Technique of Latin-American Dancing. London, Imperial Society of Teachers of Dancing, 1983.

Izumigawa, Roger. "Aloha State Games a Success." Amateur Dancers Nov/Dec 1998: 29.

Jacob, Ellen. Dancing -- A Guide for the Dancer You Can Be. Newburyport, Variety Arts 1984.

Johnson, Don Hanlon. Bone, Breath, & Gesture -- Practices of Embodiment. Berkeley, North Atlantic Books, 1995.

Jonathan. "What Is Dancesport Competitive Ballroom Dancing?" No Date. In Ballroom Dance Planet Blog. https://www.ballroomdanceplanet.com/what-is-dancesport-competitive-ballroom-dancing/. Accessed 18 August 2022.

Keogh, Justin W L et al. "Physical benefits of dancing for healthy older adults: a review." J Aging Phys Act. 2009 Oct;17(4):479-500.

Keoghan, Sarah. "Breakdancing is now an Olympic event. What will it take to win a medal?" https://www.smh.com.au/sport/breakdancing-is-now-an-olympic-sport-what-does-it-take-to-win-a-medal-20201208-p56lqp.html. Accessed 2 March 2022.

Kirchner-Bockholt, Margarete. Foundations of Curative Eurythmy. Edinburgh, Floris Books. 2005.

Kragness, Haley E. et al. Tiny dancers: Effects of musical familiarity and tempo on children's free dancing. Dev Psychol. 2022 Jul;58(7):1277-1285.

Kurath, Gertrude P. "Native American dance.No date. " https://www.britannica.com/art/Native-American-dance. Accessed 13 November 2021.

Laban, Rudoph. Schrifttanz. Wein, Universal,1928.

Laird, Walter. Technique of Latin Dancing - SUPPLEMENT. Brighton, International Dance Publications, 1997
---. Technique of Latin Dancing. London, International Dance Teachers' Association, 1964.

Lakes, Kimberley D. "Dancer Perceptions of the Cognitive, Social, Emotional, and Physical Benefits of Modern Styles of Partnered Dancing." Complement Ther Med. 2016 Jun; 26: 117–122.

"'L'Apache' (French Apache Dance) by Michael and Evita." 1 May 2015. https://youtu.be/NPShAmfCafw. Accessed 16 February 2022.

Lavelle, Doris. Latin and American Dances. London, Sir Issac Pitman & Sons, 1965.

Liiv, Helena et al. Anthropometry, somatotypes, and aerobic power in ballet, contemporary dance, and dancesport. Med Probl Perform Art. 2013 Dec; 28(4):207-11.

Malamov, Atanas G. "Benefits of Ballroom Dancing for Kids." 8 February 2020. Republished as "Create, Inspire, Dance" https://www.atanasmalamov.com/blog/benefits-of-ballroom-dancing-for-kids. Accessed 6 July 2022.

"Mambo Music Guide: A History of Mambo's Cuban Origins" 2 Nov 2021. https://www.masterclass.com/articles/mambo-music-guide#what-is-mambo. Accessed 3 December 2021.

Mann, W. Edward. Vital Energy and Health: Dr. Wilhelm Reich's Revolutionary Discoveries and Supporting Evidence. Toronto, Gagne Printing 1989 from https://archive.org/details/vitalenergy-healt0000mann/page/n3/mode/2up?view=theater. Accessed 29 June 2022.

McCabe, Teri R et al. A bibliographic review of medicine and science research in dancesport. Med Probl Perform Art. 2013 Jun; 28(2):70-9.

Merriam-Webster. "Power." 2022. https://www.merriam-webster.com/dictionary/power. Accessed 15 June 2022.

Merriam-Webster's Collegiate Dictionary (Eleventh Edition). Springfield, Merriam-Webster, 2019.

Miller, Ashley. "Natural Ways to Increase Serotonin & Endorphins." No Date. https://healthyliving.azcentral.com/dancing-release-endorphins-5764.html. Accessed 6 July 2022.

Min, Khor Su. "Olympic dream Spurs Couple." The New Paper Aug 1997.

Moore, Alex. Ballroom Dancing [Fourth Edition 1939 Reprint]. Lavergne, Pomona Press, 2006.
---. Ballroom Dancing Ninth Edition. London, A&C Black, 1986.

---. Revised Technique of Ballroom Dance Seventh Edition. Kingston-on-Thames, Alex Moore, 1962.

---. Popular Variations. Kingston on Thames, DanceSport International Ltd., 1954.

Moore, Sherry. "5 Major Prenatal Fitness Benefits That Come from Taking Ballroom Dance Lessons. 6 June 2019. https://celebrityballroomdance.com/author/sherry/. Accessed 8 July 2022.

Monte, John & Lawrence, Bobbie (Eds). The Fred Astaire Dance Book. New York, Simon & Schuster 1978.

Murray, Arthur. How to Become a Good Dancer. New York, Simon & Schuster, 1959.

---. How to Become a Good Dancer. New York, Simon & Schuster, 1942.

---. Let's Dance. New York, Arthur Murray, 1953.

---. Murray-Go-Round: The Arthur Murray Dance Book. New York Arthur Murray, 1958.

"NDCA Rules & Regulations." January 2022. https://www.ndca.org/pdf/2022%20March%20-%20Compiled%20Rule%20Book%20Master%20v2.pdf. Accessed 16 June 2022.

"NEWS & PRESS: NATIONAL Gender Neutral Announcement." 2019. https://usadance.org/news/470072/Gender-Neutral-Announcement.htm. Accessed 2 July 2022.

"Origin of Tango Rhythm." No date. http://www.waltzadventure.com/tango-discussions/origin-of-tango-rhythm/. Accessed 12 December 2021.

Orquesta América del 55. Colección Perlas Cubanas #114. 19 April 2018. https://www.youtube.com/watch?v=swiLvDLb7g8. Accessed 3 December 2021.

Paradiseresort. "SYDNEY 2000 OLYMPICS (1/6) - JOHN PAUL YOUNG - LOVE IS IN THE AIR." https://www.youtube.com/watch?v=WUKvRPHQWbA. Accessed 19 September 2022.

Patrick. K. C. "Orphans and Olympians." Dance Magazine. Feb 2002.

Penalosa, David and Greenwood, Peter. The Clave Matrix: Afro-Cuban Rhythm: its Principles and African Origins. Scott's Valley, CreateSpace Independent Publishing Platform, 2012.

Picart, Caroline Joan S. From Ballroom to DanceSport. Albany, State University of New York 2006.

Pover, Peter. "What is DanceSport?" Amateur Dancers Jan/Feb 1999:29.

Pyles, Christian. Why Isn't DanceSport an Olympic Sport? 10 June 2017. https://www.flodance.com/articles/5063980-why-isnt-dance-sport-an-olympic-sport. Accessed 27 January 2022.

Queensland Brain Institute. "Can you grow new brain cells?" 17 November 2017. https://qbi.uq.edu.au/blog/2017/11/can-you-grow-new-brain-cells. Accessed 9 July 2022.
---. "Memory and Age." No Date. https://qbi.uq.edu.au/brain-basics/memory/memory-and-age. Accessed 12 July 2022.

QuotesDisney. "The 15 Most Important Pirates of the Caribbean Quotes, According to You" 5 January 2016. https://news.disney.com/the-15-most-important-pirates-of-the-caribbean-quotes-according-to-you. Accessed 1 July 2022.

Ray, Lillian. Modern Ballroom Dancing. Chicago, Franklin Publishing Company, 1933.

Reynolds, John. Ballroom Dancing: The Romance, Rhythm and Style. Toronto, Key Porter Books Ltd 1998.

Rock & Roll Dance 1957 (American Bandstand). 7 Mar 2016. https://www.youtube.com/watch?v=xdSGjmhtaL0. Accessed 4 December 2021.

Rodrigues, Ann. "Ice Dance and DanceSport." Amateur Dancers May/June 1998: 3-5.

"Rudolph Valentino, TANGO DANCING." 13 July 2017. https://youtu.be/b_sG5vRKcB0. Accessed 16 February 2022.

Sandel, Susan L, Chaiklin, Sharon and Lohn, Ann. Foundations of Dance/Movement Therapy: The Life and Work of Marian Chace. Columbia, The American Dance Therapy Association 1993.

Sanders, Sarah G. "Dancing through pregnancy: activity guidelines for professional and recreational dancers." J Dance Med Sci. 2008;12(1):17-22.

Savoy Ballroom [Chicago]. No date. https://jazzagechicago.wordpress.com/savoy-ballroom/. Accessed 27 November 2021.

Shalvarov. Egor. "4 Reasons Why Your Child SHOULD NOT Ballroom Dance." No Date. https://www.dancecompreview.com/4-reasons-why-your-child-should-not-ballroom-dance/. Accessed 6 July 2022.

Sher, Mikc. "Stompin' at the Savoy." 17 June 2008. https://www.ebar.com/arts_&_culture///224053. Accessed 27 November 2021.

Sophia Loren - Mambo italiano. 17 May 2014. https://www.youtube.com/watch?v=XL8_WRJmFJU. Accessed 3 December 2021.

Spirov, Rangal and Chernyavska, Veronika. "5 Ways Kids Benefit From Ballroom Dance." 13 June 2020. https://www.imageballroom-dance.com/post/5-ways-kids-benefit-from-ballroom-dancing. Accessed 6 July 2022.

Stahl, Jennifer. "So You're Pregnant. Here's How to Keep Dancing Safely." 6 March 2021. Dance Magazine. https://www.dancemagazine.com/dancing-while-pregnant/. Accessed 8 July 2022.

---. "We're Born to Love Dance—Science Says So!" 19 September 2017. Dance Magazine. https://www.dancemagazine.com/why-humans-love-dance/. Accessed 17 July 2022.

Static (2021). Directed by Kenny Simmons, performances by Daniel S. Janik, Eriko Okada, Jeri Lynn Endo, Benjamin Wilkison, Shane Chisum and Setsuko Tsuchiya, K. Simmons Productions, 2021.

Steiner, Rudolf. "A Lecture on Eurythmy (GA 279)." 26 Aug 1923. https://rsarchive.org/Lectures/GA279/English/RSP1967/19230826p01.html. Accessed 29 June 2022.

Stephenson, Richard M & Iaccarino Joseph. The Complete Book of Ballroom Dancing. New York, Doubleday, 1980.

Stevenson, Dave. "History of the Canadian DanceSport Association." 2012. https://www.dancesport.ca/page6.php. Accessed 23 June 2022.

"'Tango': Corazon de Oro, A Juan Carlos Copes, La Cumparsita, Tango Barbaro." 15 December 2021. https://youtu.be/HDX0Vet61A4?t=281. Accessed 16 February 2022.

Tango, Jay. "The Greatest Dance Step Ever Invented." 12 February 2019. https://www.jaytango.com/?p=65. Accessed 26 November 2021.

"Technique Books." 2021. https://www.worlddancesport.org/WDSF/Academy/Technique_Books. Accessed 22 Sept 2021.

"TERPSIKHORE." 2017. https://www.theoi.com/Ouranios/MousaTerpsikhore.html. Accessed 21 July 2022.

That Night in Rio [1941]. Directed by Irving Cummings. Starring Don Ameche, Alice Faye and Carmen Miranda. 23 March 2011. "Chica Chica Boom Chic" clip. https://www.youtube.com/watch?v=-vt5k7qxyv8. Accessed 10 June 2022.

The Pasadena Star-News. "The musical Dodworth clan and their Pasadena legacy." 29 April 2012. https://www.pasadenastarnews.com/2012/04/29/the-musical-dodworth-clan-and-their-pasadena-legacy/. Accessed 29 May 2022.

The Spirit Moves: A History of Black Social Dance on Film, 1900–1986 (Excerpt from part 3 of the out of print DVD). A film by Mura Dehn. 9 January 2019. https://www.youtube.com/watch?v=gucZ-IXHWXQo. Accessed 3 December 2021.

The University of Queensland. "Research hits the sweet spot for healthy brains." 24 October 2016. https://hmns.uq.edu.au/article/2017/10/research-hits-sweet-spot-healthy-brains. Accessed 12 July 2022.

TheWorldGames. "The World Games 2001 in Akita (JPN)." 10 January 2021. https://www.youtube.com/watch?v=GqOkJVsQm4E. Accessed 19 September 2022.

The World Games. "DanceSport." No Date. https://www.theworldgames.org/sports/DanceSport-9. Accessed 23 June 2022.

Transatlantic Merry-Go-Round [1934]. Directed by Benjamin Stoloff. Starring Gene Raymond, Nancy Caroll and Jack Benny. 8 July

2013. https://www.youtube.com/watch?v=nOw-NjSEDus&list=RDnOw-NjSEDus&index=1. Accessed 6 Dec 2021.

Tsuchiya, Setsuko. In Search of Somatic Therapy. Honolulu, Savant Books and Publications, 2017.

United States Centers for Disease Control and Prevention. "Minorities and Women Are at Greater Risk for Alzheimer's Disease." 20 August 2019. https://www.cdc.gov/aging/publications/features/Alz-Greater-Risk.html. Accessed 9 July 2022.

---. "Physical Activity: Walking. Why Walk? Why Not!" 3 June 2022. https://www.cdc.gov/physicalactivity/walking/index.htm. Accessed 8 July 2022.

United States Social Security Administration. "How Retirement Benefits Work." No Date. https://www.ssa.gov/benefits/retirement/learn.html#h3. Accessed 9 July 2022.

USA Dance Academy. "Competitor Guide." No Date. https://usadance.org/page/CompetitorGuide. Accessed 5 November 2021.

USA Dance. "Competitor Guide." No Date. https://usadance.org/page/CompetitorGuide. Accessed 18 July 2022.

---. "DanceSport Rule Book." 2022. https://cdn.ymaws.com/us-adance.org/resource/resmgr/governance/rules/USADance-dancesportrulebook.pdf. Accessed 16 June 2022.

---. "What is DanceSport?" No date. https://usadance.org/page/WhatisDanceSport. Accessed 26 February 2022.

USISTD. International Foxtrot. 2022. https://usistd.org/syllabi-technique/international-style/international-foxtrot/. Accessed 6 June 2022.

---. International Tango. 2022. https://usistd.org/syllabi-technique/international-style/tango/. Accessed 3 June.2022.

---. International Quickstep. 2022. https://usistd.org/syllabi-technique/

international-style/international-quickstep/. Accessed 3 June 2022.
---. International Viennese Waltz. 2022. https://usistd.org/syllabi-technique/international-style/viennese-waltz/. Accessed 3 June.2022.
---. International Waltz. 2021, https://usistd.org/syllabi-technique/international-style/international-waltz/. Accessed 7 Aug.2021.

Varga, George. "All right! Elvis Presley's first 45 turns 60." 19 July 2014. https://www.sandiegouniontribune.com/entertainment/music/sdut-debut-record-by-elvis-presley-is-sixty-years-old-2014jul19-htmlstory.html, Accessed 6 December 2021.

"Western Countries 2022." No Date. https://worldpopulationreview.com/country-rankings/western-countries. Accessed 21 July 2022.

"What is Ballroom Dancing?" No date. https://www.adancetoremembertx.com/what-is-ballroom-dancing. Accessed 26 February 2022.

Whitehouse, Mary. "The Tao of the Body" in Johnson, Don Hanlon (ed) Bone, Breath, & Gesture: Practices of Embodiment. Berkeley, North Atlantic Books 1995.

World DanceSport Federation. "About DanceSport." 2022. https://www.worlddancesport.org/About. Accessed 27 January 2022.
---. "Breaking officially added to Olympic Games Paris 2024." https://www.worlddancesport.org/News/WDSF/Breaking_officially_added_to_Olympic_Games_Paris_2024-3147. Accessed 2 March 2022.
---. "DanceSport Disciplines." 2022. https://www.worlddancesport.org/About/Dance_Styles/DanceSport_Disciplines. Accessed 13 August 2022.
---. "DanceSport for All!" 2022. https://www.worlddancesport.org/about/all. Accessed 2 March 2022.
---. "Issue 2015/02: Not In Tokyo 2020." 29 June 2015. https://www.worlddancesport.org/Media/Press/Release/Issue_201502_Not_In_Tokyo_2020-1864. Accessed 27 June 2022.

---. "rules." 2022. htttps://www.worlddancesport.org/rule/competition/general. Accessed 4 Oct 2021.
---. "syllabus." 2022. https://www.worlddancesport.org/rule/athlete/competition/syllabus. Accessed 18 June 2022.

Wright, Gregory. "Ame-no-Uzume." 19 November 2021. https://mythopedia.com/topics/ame-no-uzume. Accessed 21 July 2022.

If you enjoyed *The Power of Partner Dance* consider *In Search of Somatic Therapy* by the same author

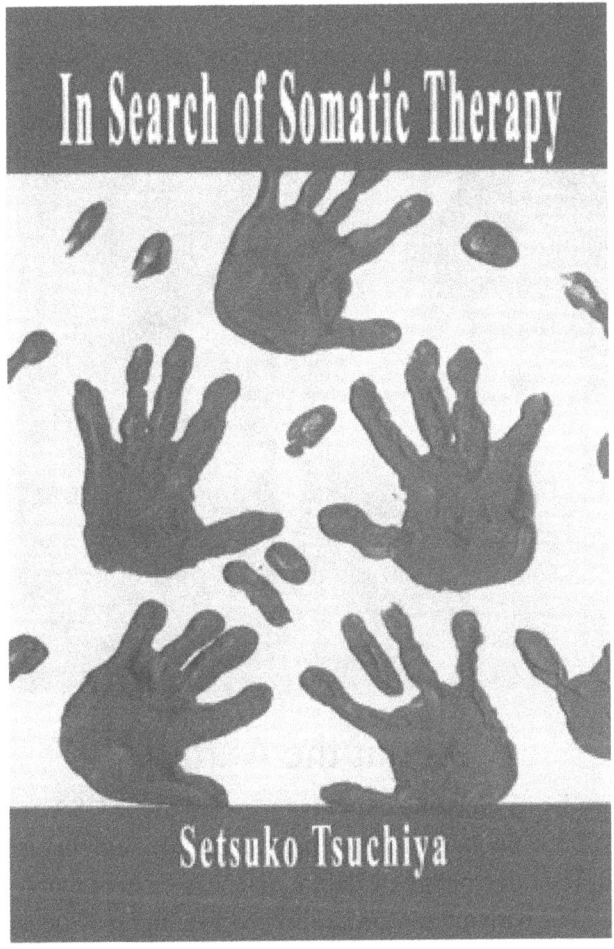

What is somatic therapy? Is it about somatic therapy (psychological "talk therapy" that surrounds somatic stimulation) or somatic therapy (the somatic stimulation itself)? Do the different forms of somatic experience, e.g. massage, dance, singing, acupuncture, acupressure and biofeedback have anything in common other than afterwards talking about the experience? The author, a registered Hawaii massage therapist documents her journey in search of somatic therapy and the surprises that revealed themselves along the way.

About the Author

Originally from Japan, **Setsuko Tsuchiya** traveled to the USA and earned a BA in Liberal Arts from Thomas Edison University while studying medical massage therapy at Hawaii College of Health Sciences. After completing her undergraduate studies with a focus on dance, and becoming a licensed medical massage therapist, she began wondering if there might be a truly fundamental somatic (body) basis for the burgeoning number of therapies and dance organizations, one independent of language and applicable to all cultures in this increasingly globalized world. Author, dancer, actress and somatic therapist, her belief that partner dancing is at the heart of the power of dance is the basis of this work. "The Power of Partner Dance" is taken, in part, from her PhD dissertation entitled, "The Power of Partnered Ballroom Dance " in fulfillment of a PhD in Performing Arts in Ballroom and Latin Dance Performance.

Index

A

abakuá, 33
abbreviations, 49–50, 71, 74
abdominal, 39, 80–81
abilities, 107, 155, 183
ability, 111, 126, 146, 168
accident, 107
accidents, 165
accomplishment, 169
acrobatic, 39, 129
acrobatics, 37
activity, 8–9, 11, 126, 130, 136, 141, 155, 157, 160, 162–163, 166, 174, 190
actor, 21, 26, 31
actress, 21, 150
actualization, 169
actualizing, 141, 175
adaptation, 87
adjudicated, 66
Adjudicator, 6, 19
adjudicator, 152
Adult, 167
adult, 5, 158, 167
adulthood, 157
Adults, 5, 156
adults, 146, 156–157, 162, 166

adverse, 162
advertisers, 130
adynamic, 36, 57, 78
aesthetic, 13
aestheticized, 129
affectionados, 92
Africa, 33, 63, 75
aggression, 155
agility, 164
Aida, 97
Akita, 109, 125
Albert, 4, 6, 19, 31–33, 36, 43, 49, 52–53, 59–60, 64, 66, 69, 72, 76, 85, 88–89, 94, 117, 119–120, 139
Alemana, 77, 95–98
alignment, 25, 50, 71, 74, 81
Aloha, 108, 123–124
Alzheimer, 164, 167
amalgamate, 174
amalgamated, 25, 59, 61, 81, 118
amalgamation, 57, 59–60
amalgamations, 27, 48, 61, 74, 177
América, 38
analysis, 168
Andalusian, 20
ankle, 60, 66, 119

INDEX

ankles, 22, 50, 59, 117
Anthroposophical, 137
anxiety, 129, 156, 164, 168
Apache, 21
appearance, 19, 30, 37, 52–53, 71–73, 132, 166
Appel, 84–87
appreciation, 159
archetypal, 156
ardor, 126
Argentine, 8, 20–22, 63
Argentino, 20
aristocratic, 57, 117
artistic, 113, 132
artists, 126
Astaire, 1, 25–27, 29, 39, 73, 79
Athans, 6
Athlete, 7, 164
athlete, 146
Athletes, 10, 106
athletes, 3, 14, 107–108, 120, 124, 126, 145, 151–152, 154, 174, 189–190
athletic, 39, 105, 107, 151, 174, 191
athletically, 159
athleticism, 120, 129
attentiveness, 73, 138
attire, 132
attitude, 33, 36, 169
audience, 54, 57, 65, 87, 90–91, 124, 126, 129, 145–146, 148, 155–156, 178–181, 183
audiences, 57, 79, 91, 96, 108, 190
Australia, 187
Austria, 55
Austrian, 16
Authentic, 113
authentic, 113, 150
authentically, 140, 175
awareness, 134, 140, 158–160

B

Bachata, 8
Ballet, 114, 124
ballet, 8, 92, 139, 174–176, 179
Ballroom, 2–4, 6–9, 13, 16, 20, 22, 29, 31–32, 36–41, 45–46, 48–62, 64–66, 70–73, 83, 86, 92, 103, 105, 109, 116–118, 123–126, 129, 136, 143–145, 151, 157–159, 169, 173, 177–178, 181–182
ballroom, 1, 3, 5–10, 13–19, 21–22, 24–26, 29–33, 36, 39, 41, 46, 50–51, 54–55, 58, 60, 62–63, 65, 70, 75, 80, 83, 85, 90, 92, 108–109, 111, 117, 123, 125–131, 133–134, 146, 148–153, 156–159, 163–164, 167, 169, 173–184, 187–193

Setsuko Tsuchiya

INDEX

ballrooms, 10, 30, 38, 79, 84, 150
ballroomstyle, 14
Banderillas, 84, 86
Bandstand, 1, 42–43
bandstand, 39
bantu, 34
Barbossa, 147
barrier, 190
barriers, 9, 151, 153
Barrio, 20
barrios, 63
Bartlett, 168
Basse, 14
Baxter, 159
Bebop, 89, 92
beginner, 31–32, 35, 55, 60
Beginners, 173
beginners, 35, 155
Belgian, 20
benefactors, 160
beneficial, 162, 164, 168
Benesh, 115
Berlin, 22
Bigelow, 159
Blackmore, 168
bloomers, 22
Blyth, 21
Bockholt, 138
Bolero, 8, 29, 36, 39, 41, 104, 173
Bon, 5, 112
Bonner, 131
Boogie, 89, 92
boop, 77
bopping, 42

Bose, 150
Bossanova, 29
Boston, 17, 19, 23, 30–31
Bota, 82
boundaries, 7, 156, 159
Bowery, 21
Bradley, 46
Brady, 42
Brain, 168
brain, 167–168
brains, 167–168, 180
brassiere, 22
Brazil, 16, 119
Brazilian, 38, 41, 79
Brazilians, 79
Breakdance, 10
Breakdancing, 10, 190
breakdancing, 190
breath, 139
breathingPage, 191
Bresilien, 38, 79
Bresilienne, 21
Broadway, 25, 156
Bronze, 62, 72, 104, 184
brothels, 15, 18
BUDOKAN, 4
Buenos, 20, 63
bull, 83–84, 87
bullfight, 83–84, 86
bullfighting, 83, 85, 120
Bunny, 23

C

Cabaret, 181–182
cabaret, 149

INDEX

CADA, 123
Cakewalk, 18–19, 57–58
California, 6
Camarlinghi, 6
Canadian, 123
Cancao, 41
Cape, 84, 86–87
cape, 83–84, 87–88
cardiovascular, 157, 163–164
career, 1, 23, 42–43
Caribbean, 37, 147
Carioca, 79
carioca, 39
Carmen, 39, 80
Carnaval, 119
Carnival, 79
Carringford, 31
Catalan, 34
CBM, 36, 56, 60–61, 64, 76, 86, 90
CBMP, 50, 56, 60–61, 64, 76, 86–87, 90
Cha, 1, 5, 8, 16, 25, 27, 29, 37–39, 41, 70, 80–81, 92–99, 104–105, 119, 173, 184
cha, 37
Chace, 113, 128, 140–141, 175
Chaiklin, 128, 141
Championship, 48, 104–105, 184
championship, 66, 118, 176
Championships, 3–4, 107
championships, 152
Chang, 6
charanga, 38
charangas, 37
Charleston, 58, 60
Chaudhari, 131
chest, 54, 85
Chicago, 40
chickenskin, 150, 178
childbirth, 163
childhood, 146, 159, 161
circulation, 138
Clark, 1, 43
Clarke, 17–18, 40, 46, 53, 57–58, 60, 63, 83, 85, 88, 180
claves, 35
Clement, 18, 57
Cognitive, 167
cognitive, 158, 164, 168
cognitively, 158
coherent, 174
cohesive, 45, 183
Cole, 26
Collegiate, 24, 178
Colombia, 125
Competition, 75, 107, 180
competition, 4, 6, 10–14, 30, 32–33, 36, 42–43, 48, 51, 56, 62, 66, 76, 83, 86, 88, 90–91, 95, 97, 99, 104–106, 109, 113–114, 118–120, 123–125, 129, 139, 144, 149–150, 152, 154–155, 160, 164–165, 167, 169, 174, 178, 180–183, 189–190, 192
Competitions, 107

competitions, 51, 54, 62,
  65–66, 91, 95, 106,
  108–109, 116–118, 128,
  151, 154, 159, 180, 182
Competitor, 8, 173, 181–182,
  184
competitor, 2–3, 76, 95, 117,
  124, 174
Competitors, 109, 132, 184
competitors, 1, 4, 7, 10, 48,
  50, 52, 66, 74, 81, 88,
  104, 106–108, 119, 124,
  128, 130–132, 152, 155,
  165, 178
Comte, 144
confidence, 143, 157–158
Conga, 24–25
Connection, 76, 119
connection, 53, 69, 72–73,
  89–91, 95, 112, 114, 142,
  163, 184
connectivity, 134
consciously, 156–157
consciousness, 138
continuity, 27, 180
Contredanse, 14
Corset, 22
Corta, 80
Corte, 64
corte, 33, 63
costume, 22, 154
costumed, 79
costumes, 3, 18, 112, 159
costuming, 128–130, 152
cotillion, 14
cotillions, 14

Coup, 84, 86
COVID, 14, 130, 166, 176,
  190
CPP, 82
Crawford, 26
Criss, 82
criteria, 9, 12, 145
criterion, 51
Crosby, 26
Crozier, 63
Cuba, 2, 16, 33–34, 36, 63,
  75
Cuban, 2, 34–38, 41, 69–70,
  75–76, 78, 90, 92, 95,
  97–98
Cubano, 34, 37
Cucarachas, 78
Cugat, 34
Curative, 138
curiosity, 134
curious, 97
cyclical, 138
Czech, 30

D

Dancer, 2, 24–25, 105, 178
dancer, 1, 21, 26, 40, 48, 50,
  74, 77, 84–85, 93, 115,
  130, 142, 146, 149–150,
  176, 179–180
Dancers, 7, 37, 63, 103, 105,
  107, 123, 142, 174
dancers, 1, 10, 14, 20,
  22–23, 26, 37–39, 45, 49,
  53, 56, 62–63, 72–75,

78–80, 92, 97, 107, 114–115, 124, 127, 130–131, 136, 140–144, 148–150, 152, 156, 158–159, 165, 167, 169, 173–177, 179, 189
DanceSport, 3, 6–7, 9–12, 19, 48, 50–51, 53, 56, 58, 64, 66, 72, 75–76, 95, 103–109, 111, 114, 116–120, 123–134, 136, 139, 145–146, 150–156, 159–160, 164, 174–178, 180–184, 188–190
Dancesport, 93, 181
Deasy, 23
deconditioning, 167
deference, 145
degenerative, 164
Dementia, 168
dementia, 164, 167–168
dementias, 167
dePage, 141
Deplacement, 84
deportment, 17
dess, 188
deux, 17, 19, 55
development, 17, 24, 30–31, 55, 105, 143, 158, 162
Devotion, 191
devotion, 149, 192
diabetes, 164
digestive, 138
Disco, 43, 89, 128
discrimination, 149, 154
Displacement, 86

diversity, 114, 139
DMT, 137, 191
Doble, 8, 16, 20, 69–71, 83–88, 93, 105, 119–120, 173, 184
Dodworth, 16
Dolly, 31
Dominican, 41
Doucet, 6
drama, 85, 88, 119, 126, 192
dramatically, 87
dreamdancing, 60
DSC, 11–12, 107
Duisburg, 125
Duke, 89
dysfunctional, 140

E

eastern, 34
Ecart, 84
Egyptian, 144
elegance, 19, 58
elegant, 165
Ellen, 178
Ellington, 89
emotion, 53, 124, 144, 148, 156, 192
emotions, 131, 137, 139, 141, 146, 148
Empathy, 146
empathy, 141, 146, 148, 157, 189
endorphins, 142, 159
endurance, 133, 144, 164
energy, 79, 111–113, 115,

INDEX

124, 135, 141–142, 159, 163, 184
Enge, 24
Engel, 27
England, 1–2, 21, 40, 58, 84, 88
equality, 152
equitable, 108, 145
erotic, 118
eroticism, 149
eurhythmy, 136
eurythmic, 128, 169
Eurythmy, 138
eurythmy, 135, 137–138, 144
Evans, 124
Exhibition, 108, 124
exhibition, 21, 83, 85, 124
exhibitions, 21, 124
experimentation, 133, 158
explanations, 24
exploration, 188
extremism, 120

F

fads, 43
Fallaway, 57, 84, 87, 89
fallaway, 49, 76
fantasy, 124
Farol, 86–88
fashionable, 63
Faye, 26
feet, 35, 46, 49–50, 52, 54, 64, 86
Festival, 108, 112, 124
festival, 112

festivals, 5
fetus, 162, 169
fitness, 9, 11, 141, 143, 151, 158
flair, 77
Flamenca, 20, 34
Flamenco, 20, 34, 84, 86
Flamingo, 88
Fleckerl, 66
Fleet, 26
Flexibility, 157
flexibility, 31, 52, 58, 71, 114, 128, 141, 157, 163, 192
flirtation, 119
flirting, 93
flirty, 38
Fogos, 82
follower, 52, 71, 77–78, 91, 97–99, 114, 131, 146–147
Followers, 52, 72
footankle, 85
Foote, 21
footturn, 50
Footwork, 64
footwork, 25, 27, 35, 50, 52, 56, 59, 61, 71, 76, 81, 84–85, 94, 96, 112, 140
forgiveness, 157
FoxTrot, 63
Foxtrot, 8, 18–19, 23, 25, 27, 29, 31–32, 40–41, 53, 57–60, 64, 103, 105, 117–118, 173, 184
foxtrot, 31
Francisco, 23, 40

INDEX

Franz, 4, 6, 19, 31–33, 36, 43, 49, 52–53, 55–56, 59–60, 64, 66, 69–72, 74–78, 80–81, 85–86, 88–90, 94–95, 117, 119–120, 139
Fregolina, 84, 86–88
Freud, 191
friendship, 131, 146, 189

G

Galician, 34
Garber, 137
garters, 22
Geisenhainer, 6
Gender, 133, 145–146, 149, 152
gender, 9, 108, 145–154
gentleman, 51, 84
gentlemanly, 142
gestational, 139
Gipsy, 34
Gleissner, 137
globalization, 153
Glover, 124
GNC, 152
goal, 52, 71, 176, 184
goals, 152
Godel, 153
gooey, 69, 72–73, 76, 95, 119, 184
gooeyness, 49, 69
Gorman, 43
Greece, 137
Grizzly, 23

Grove, 34
Guapacha, 96

H

habanera, 23
Haiti, 36
Haitians, 36
Haley, 42
happiness, 112, 139
Harlem, 37
Harmony, 137
harmony, 135, 180
Havana, 23, 34, 37–38
Hawaii, 4, 6, 84, 123–124, 131, 165, 176
Hawkins, 6
hazards, 157
Hegemann, 11
Henie, 26
Herbison, 124
Hesitation, 21, 57
Hesitations, 30
Hill, 17
hill, 61
HipHop, 128
Hitchcock, 150
Ho, 6
Hoch, 161
holistically, 178
Hollywood, 63, 156
Honolulu, 4, 108, 124, 131, 165
hormones, 148
Howard, 116
HT, 56

INDEX

Huit, 84, 86–87
humanism, 189
Humphreys, 46
Hutchinson, 115

I

Iacarrino, 39
Iaccarino, 13–21, 23–24, 26–27, 30–39, 41–43, 55, 58, 64, 79–81, 86, 89, 92–94
IDSF, 9–12, 106–107, 116, 123, 125, 129, 151
IDTA, 116–117, 127
illusion, 60–62, 64, 66, 118, 144
IMG, 12, 125
immortality, 45, 192
India, 144
Indian, 18
Indie, 150
infant, 161
Infants, 5, 161
infants, 162
injuries, 165
injury, 157
Ipanema, 41
Irving, 22
ISDT, 45
ISTD, 40, 46, 48–65, 69–78, 80–82, 85–91, 93–99, 103–105, 109, 116–118, 127, 129, 177
Italian, 37
Italiano, 37

IWGA, 108
Izumigawa, 108, 124, 131

J

Janik, 4
Japan, 3, 5, 99, 109, 112, 117, 125, 143, 153
Japanization, 153
Jardin, 31
Jitterbug, 5, 24–25, 40, 43, 88–89, 92
JIVE, 88
Jive, 8, 16, 40, 43, 70, 88–92, 99, 105, 120, 173, 184
Johnson, 113
Joint, 157
joint, 125, 166
joints, 157, 163
Jolicoeur, 6
Joplin, 18
joy, 5, 62, 134, 139, 159

K

Kaohsiung, 125
Keeler, 26
Kenyon, 27
Keogh, 166
Keoghan, 12
Khor, 126
kindness, 159
kinesthesia, 140
Kinesthetic, 114
kinesthetic, 52, 71, 114, 140, 175

INDEX

Kirchner, 138
Kozinska, 6
Kragness, 160
Kurath, 15

L

Laban, 115
Labanotation, 115
Laird, 117
Lamour, 26
Lancers, 14, 17
Langer, 148
Lanner, 55
LaPatin, 6
Lapatin, 93
LatinAmerican, 6, 73, 90–91, 105
Lavelle, 2, 48
Leader, 99
leader, 14, 32, 37, 52, 56, 71, 79, 82, 89, 97, 99, 114, 131, 146–147
Leialoha, 6
Lew, 34
Lewandowski, 6
LGBTQ, 145
ligament, 157
ligaments, 166
Liiv, 157
Limon, 124
Lindbergh, 40
Lindy, 24, 27, 29–30, 38, 40, 43
LOD, 50, 56, 61, 64, 81
Lynnsay, 6

lyrics, 42, 139

M

Madrid, 34
maenad, 137
Malamov, 158
Mambo, 8, 24–25, 27, 29, 36–39, 41, 92, 94, 104, 173
mambo, 36
Mann, 113
manners, 13, 15, 176
Maranda, 39
Marceau, 139
Mariusz, 6
Matador, 84
matador, 83
Maypole, 82
McAllister, 15
McCabe, 157
McCormack, 125
Medalist, 72
medalist, 13
melodrama, 129
Meredith, 6, 93
Merengue, 8, 25, 29, 41
Mexico, 14–15
Miller, 159
milonga, 23
milongas, 32
mime, 144
mimetic, 136
mimic, 161
Min, 126
Minorities, 167

INDEX

Minuet, 14
minuet, 17
Miranda, 80
Miwa, 6
Mo, 112
moiety, 14
Monte, 27, 29
Moore, 2, 46, 52–55, 57, 61, 64–66, 116, 118, 163, 166, 177
motivation, 143, 158
Mousai, 188
Mouvet, 20
movie, 1, 25–26, 42, 79, 147, 149–150, 156, 169, 174
movies, 18, 25–26, 34, 50, 148, 150, 192
Murray, 1, 6, 23–27, 29, 73, 147
muscular, 138
musculature, 148
Muses, 180, 188
musicality, 54, 72

N

Nachantz, 16
Nagano, 12
nationalism, 153
nationally, 152
Navajo, 125
NDCA, 104, 106–107, 164, 182
neck, 50, 85
neurobiologist, 167

neurogenesis, 168
neurons, 168
newcomers, 48
newspapers, 15
Nichols, 48
Nightclub, 7
nonverbal, 113, 158
Notation, 115
notation, 45, 48, 51–52, 54, 71, 74, 77, 93, 115, 176, 178
notational, 49–50, 74, 115
Nova, 41–42
NST, 50
nurturing, 139

O

Okazaki, 6
Olympic, 3, 9–12, 105–108, 117, 123–125, 127–130, 132–133, 136, 145–146, 150–152, 154, 176, 189–190
Olympics, 3, 9–12, 108–109, 124–126, 129–130, 134, 146, 154, 189–190
Orquesta, 38

P

palos, 20, 34
Papanti, 17
Paralympic, 108, 124
Paris, 10–11, 20–21, 40, 179, 190
partnerdance, 127

INDEX

Partnership, 111, 141, 143, 159, 189
partnership, 8, 14, 60, 107, 111–112, 114, 120, 128, 134, 141–144, 146, 158, 160–161, 164–165, 167, 174, 183, 191, 193
partnerships, 114, 141, 176
Pasadena, 16
paseillo, 83
Passe, 84, 86–87
passion, 75, 79, 119, 134, 156, 169
Pavanes, 14
Peabody, 23, 29–32, 58, 104
Pearson, 49
pelvic, 81
Penalosa, 34
perceptions, 143
perceptive, 140
Petrides, 2, 48
petticoats, 22
Philadelphia, 1, 42
physique, 54, 73
Picador, 84
Picard, 144, 154
Picart, 9, 11–12, 129–132, 146–151, 154–156
pictograms, 45, 49
Pilobolus, 124
pioneering, 1–2
pioneers, 1, 128
Pique, 84, 86
Placid, 3
Planet, 181
Plato, 136

poise, 13, 25, 27, 50, 128
Poland, 125
Polka, 17, 19, 27, 30
polka, 30
Portuguese, 18
posture, 85, 107, 120, 128, 134, 141, 157, 163–164
postures, 17
Pover, 105–106, 123, 126
Powell, 26
PP, 50, 81–82
Prado, 1, 37
Pregnancy, 162–163
pregnancy, 162, 164
Prenatal, 163
prenatal, 163
preOlympic, 108
Presley, 42
preteen, 5
Prevention, 162, 167
primitivism, 156
procreative, 138
Promenade, 86–87, 95
promenade, 49–50, 74, 76
psyche, 113, 139
PubMed, 166
Puente, 37
Pyles, 9
Pythagoras, 135, 137–138
Pythagorean, 138

Q
Quadrilles, 14, 17
Queensland, 168
Quickstep, 8, 53, 55, 58,

INDEX

60–63, 65–66, 105, 118,
   173, 184
Quinn, 34

R
racial, 154
radicalized, 146
Ragtime, 20
ragtime, 18–19, 58
Ranas, 20
reawakened, 140
reawakens, 175
recovery, 133, 167
reflexes, 161
Reich, 191
Reichean, 113
rejection, 79, 119
relationship, 10, 159
relationships, 9, 11,
   142–143, 158, 174
relaxation, 5, 93, 143
resilience, 157
resiliency, 162
retirement, 165
Reynolds, 16, 18, 48, 57,
   61–64, 66, 79, 81, 85,
   89–90, 92, 107, 117–119,
   126–127, 176
Rhodes, 37
Rhumba, 34
Rhythmic, 161
rhythmic, 24, 89, 93, 132,
   138, 141, 160–161
rhythmical, 138
rhythmically, 8, 138

Richardson, 45
Rio, 26, 39, 79–80
Ririe, 124
Robertson, 6
Rodrigues, 107, 123, 145
Rogers, 26
Romain, 2, 48
Romance, 48, 117
romance, 117, 156
Romani, 20
romantic, 36, 151
Roseland, 32
Rumba, 2, 5, 8, 16, 20,
   24–25, 27, 29, 33–36,
   38–39, 41, 69–70, 75–77,
   79, 81, 93–95, 99,
   104–105, 119, 173, 184
rumba, 33

S
safety, 16, 130, 163
Salsa, 8, 29, 128
Salvador, 88
Samba, 8, 16, 24–27, 29, 34,
   38–39, 41, 69–71, 79–83,
   86, 92, 99, 105, 119, 173,
   184
samba, 39
Sanctioned, 109
sanctioned, 106, 151
Sandel, 128
Sanders, 162
Savion, 124
Savoy, 39–40
Sawyer, 34

INDEX

Schmais, 128, 141
Schottische, 19, 24
scientific, 161, 166
sensation, 112–113, 159
sensations, 161
sensory, 158
sensual, 36, 57, 75
sensuality, 126
sensually, 33
sensuous, 36
Separation, 86–87
sexuality, 152, 154
sexualized, 63
sexually, 63, 75
Shalvarov, 159
Sher, 40
Shimazaki, 6
Shinto, 188
Shrifttanz, 115
Sica, 37
Silvester, 46
Simmons, 46
skaters, 3, 107
Skating, 108, 183
skating, 32, 107, 127, 132, 182, 189
Slezakova, 24
slowslow, 30
SlowWaltz, 17, 30
Smith, 6, 46
Snowden, 40
socialization, 142, 153, 155, 164
socialize, 40, 165, 167
socially, 15, 22, 55, 58, 143–144, 158

sociopolitical, 130
soirees, 85
Somatic, 134, 145
somatic, 135, 191
Sorrento, 37
soul, 136, 138
souls, 16, 126
Sousa, 19
Spain, 16, 20, 34, 84–85
spectators, 4, 14, 96, 108, 124
Spencer, 48
Spheres, 137
spice, 93
Spiral, 36, 78, 95, 97
spiral, 76–77, 97–98, 138
spiritual, 135, 138, 142, 188
spirituality, 142, 169, 188
spiritually, 188, 192
Spirov, 158
sprain, 166
Stahl, 162, 180
stamina, 52, 72, 88, 128, 141
Starks, 113, 140
Steiner, 137–138
Stephenson, 13–21, 23–24, 26–27, 30–39, 41–43, 55, 58, 64, 79–81, 86, 89, 92–94
Stevenson, 39, 123
stimulation, 161
stimuli, 148
Strauss, 55
strength, 52, 72, 128, 141–142, 144, 157, 163, 166–167

INDEX

Su, 126
Sunnyvale, 40
sway, 25, 27, 50, 52, 56, 66, 76, 80, 86
Swayze, 37
Swivels, 91
Sydney, 48
Syllabi, 30
syllabi, 24–25, 27, 29–30, 36, 42, 46, 73–75, 103–105, 112, 116–117, 176–177
Syllabus, 105–106, 116, 184
syllabus, 9, 46, 48, 57, 62, 74, 84, 99, 103, 105, 109, 177

T

Taiwan, 125
TANGO, 63
Tango, 5, 8, 18, 20–27, 29–30, 32–33, 38, 40–41, 52–53, 62–65, 79, 103, 105, 118, 150, 173, 184
tango, 23
Tangos, 20, 32, 63
Tao, 113
Techman, 23
Technique, 2, 46, 48–62, 64–65, 69–78, 80–82, 85–91, 93–99, 106, 116–118, 129, 177
technique, 2, 52, 71, 77, 95, 128–129, 149–150
teenagers, 42

Teens, 5
Telemark, 84
tempo, 19, 21, 23, 31, 41, 55–56, 64, 75, 80, 93, 128
tension, 64, 90, 118, 149, 157
Terpsichore, 188
TERPSIKHORE, 188
Therapy, 113, 128, 134, 137, 145, 191
therapy, 135, 137, 191
Throwaway, 91
tic, 81, 179
Tipple, 62
toddler, 155, 160
Toddlers, 160
toddlers, 160–162
Tokyo, 3–4, 12, 134
Tomoko, 6
topline, 119
Toreador, 84
Torero, 84
torero, 83, 87
toreros, 83
Torres, 37
torso, 50, 72, 77, 85, 90, 95, 115, 176
Tropicana, 37
truth, 120, 155
Tsuchiya, 1–2, 4–5, 14, 16, 39, 48, 52, 69, 71–72, 105–108, 116, 134–135, 145, 148
Tsukioka, 6
Turkey, 23
Twostep, 23
Tynegate, 46

INDEX

U

Underwater, 1
unpartnered, 117, 125
USA, 1–2, 4, 6–7, 10, 13–14, 16, 19, 27, 29, 31, 34, 37, 40–41, 45, 63, 103–109, 117, 123, 125, 130–131, 151–152, 164, 173, 177, 181–182, 184, 189
USABDA, 108, 123–124
USDSC, 106
USISTD, 48, 55, 59–60, 64, 103–104, 117

V

Valentino, 63
Valse, 17, 19, 55
Varga, 42
Varsovienne, 24
vaudeville, 18–19, 21, 31, 58
veneer, 57, 117
vibration, 135, 144
vibrations, 135
victims, 130
videotaping, 50
Vienna, 55
Viennese, 8, 16–17, 29, 33, 40–41, 55, 64–67, 103, 105, 118, 173, 184
Volta, 16, 80, 82
Voltas, 81–82
voodoo, 36

W

Waltz, 5, 8, 16–17, 19, 21, 23–25, 27, 29–30, 33, 35–36, 40–41, 53, 55–58, 62–67, 80, 103, 105, 117–118, 173, 184
waltz, 16–17, 19
waltzen, 55
Waltzes, 55
waltzes, 33
warmup, 163
Washington, 4
WD, 11–12, 107
WDC, 127
WDO, 182
WDSF, 9–12, 105–106, 116–117, 125, 127–128, 150–153, 181–182, 189
Webb, 42
Welk, 1, 43
WFIL, 42
Whappacha, 96
Wheelchair, 128
wheelchair, 191
wheelchairs, 128
Whisk, 57
Whitehouse, 113, 140–141
widdershins, 15
Woodbury, 124
Woogie, 89, 92
Worthen, 131
Wright, 188
Wrocław, 125
WWII, 30

Y

Yanscri, 31
YMCA, 6
York, 15–16, 18–21, 23, 31,
　37, 39, 58, 96
Yorkers, 22
Youth, 168
youth, 11–12, 16, 190
Yuki, 6

Z

Zakrzewski, 6
Zealand, 187

Consider these other fine books from Savant Books and Publications and it's imprint Aignos Publishing

Essay, Essay, Essay by Yasuo Kobachi
Aloha from Coffee Island by Walter Miyanari
Footprints, Smiles and Little White Lies by Daniel S. Janik
The Illustrated Middle Earth by Daniel S. Janik
Last and Final Harvest by Daniel S. Janik
A Whale's Tale by Daniel S. Janik
Tropic of California by R. Page Kaufman
Tropic of California (the companion music CD) by R. Page Kaufman
The Village Curtain by Tony Tame
Dare to Love in Oz by William Maltese
The Interzone by Tatsuyuki Kobayashi
Today I Am a Man by Larry Rodness
The Bahrain Conspiracy by Bentley Gates
Called Home by Gloria Schumann
First Breath edited by Z. M. Oliver
The Jumper Chronicles by W. C. Peever
William Maltese's Flicker - #1 Book of Answers by William Maltese
My Unborn Child by Orest Stocco
Last Song of the Whales by Four Arrows
Perilous Panacea by Ronald Klueh
Falling but Fulfilled by Zachary M. Oliver
Mythical Voyage by Robin Ymer
Hello, Norma Jean by Sue Dolleris
Charlie No Face by David B. Seaburn
Number One Bestseller by Brian Morley
My Two Wives and Three Husbands by S. Stanley Gordon
In Dire Straits by Jim Currie
Wretched Land by Mila Komarnisky
Who's Killing All the Lawyers? by A. G. Hayes
Ammon's Horn by G. Amati
Wavelengths edited by Zachary M. Oliver
Communion by Jean Blasiar and Jonathan Marcantoni
The Oil Man by Leon Puissegur
Random Views of Asia from the Mid-Pacific by William E. Sharp
The Isla Vista Crucible by Reilly Ridgell
Blood Money by Scott Mastro

Setsuko Tsuchiya

In the Himalayan Nights by Anoop Chandola
On My Behalf by Helen Doan
Chimney Bluffs by David B. Seaburn
The Loons by Sue Dolleris
Light Surfer by David Allan Williams
The Judas List by A. G. Hayes
Path of the Templar—Book 2 of The Jumper Chronicles by W. C. Peever
The Desperate Cycle by Tony Tame
Shutterbug by Buz Sawyer
Blessed are the Peacekeepers by Tom Donnelly and Mike Munger
Bellwether Messages edited by D. S. Janik
The Turtle Dances by Daniel S. Janik
The Lazarus Conspiracies by Richard Rose
Purple Haze by George B. Hudson
Imminent Danger by A. G. Hayes
Lullaby Moon (CD) by Malia Elliott of Leon & Malia
Volutions edited by Suzanne Langford
In the Eyes of the Son by Hans Brinckmann
The Hanging of Dr. Hanson by Bentley Gates
Flight of Destiny by Francis Powell
Elaine of Corbenic by Tima Z. Newman
Ballerina Birdies by Marina Yamamoto
More More Time by David B. Seabird
Crazy Like Me by Erin Lee
Cleopatra Unconquered by Helen R. Davis
Valedictory by Daniel Scott
The Chemical Factor by A. G. Hayes
Quantum Death by A. G. Hayes and Raymond Gaynor
Big Heaven by Charlotte Hebert
Captain Riddle's Treasure by GV Rama Rao
All Things Await by Seth Clabough
Tsunami Libido by Cate Burns
Finding Kate by A. G. Hayes
The Adventures of Purple Head, Buddha Monkey... by Erik/Forest Bracht
In the Shadows of My Mind by Andrew Massie
The Gumshoe by Richard Rose
In Search of Somatic Therapy by Setsuko Tsuchiya
Cereus by Z. Roux
The Solar Triangle by A. G. Hayes
Shadow and Light edited by Helen R. Davis
A Real Daughter by Lynne McKelvey
StoryTeller by Nicholas Bylotas
Bo Henry at Three Forks by Daniel Bradford

The Power of Dance

Kindred edited by Gary "Doc" Krinberg
Cleopatra Victorious by Helen R. Davis
The Dark Side of Sunshine by Paul Guzzo
Cazadores de Libros Perdidos by German William Cabasssa Barber [Spanish]
The Desert and the City by Derek Bickerton
The Overnight Family Man by Paul Guzzo
There is No Cholera in Zimbabwe by Zachary M. Oliver
John Doe by Buz Sawyers
The Piano Tuner's Wife by Jean Yamasaki Toyama
An Aura of Greatness by Brendan P. Burns
Polonio Pass by Doc Krinberg
Iwana by Alvaro Leiva
University and King by Jeffrey Ryan Long
The Surreal Adventures of Dr. Mingus by Jesus Richard Felix Rodriguez
Letters by Buz Sawyers
In the Heart of the Country by Derek Bickerton
El Camino De Regreso by Maricruz Acuna [Spanish]
Prepositions by Jean Yamasaki Toyama
Deep Slumber of Dogs by Doc Krinberg
Navel of the Sea by Elizabeth McKague
Entwined edited by Gary "Doc" Krinberg
Critical Writing: Stories as Phenomena by Jamie Dela Cruz
Truth and Tell Travel the Solar System by Helen R. Davis
Saddam's Parrot by Jim Currie
Beneath Them by Natalie Roers
Chang the Magic Cat by A. G. Hayes
Illegal by E. M. Duesel
Island Wildlife: Exiles, Expats and Exotic Others by Robert Friedman
The Winter Spider by Doc Krinberg
The Princess in My Head by J. G. Matheny
Comic Crusaders by Richard Rose
I'll Remember by Clif McCrady
The City and the Desert by Derek Bickerton
The Edge of Madness by Raymond Gaynor
'Til Then Our Written Love Will Have to Do by Cheri Woods
Aloha La'a Kea edited by Robert "Uhene" Maikai
Hawaii Kids Music Vol 1 by Leon and Malia
William Maltese's Flicker - #2 Book of Ascendency by William Maltese
Retribution by Richard Rose
Shep's Adventures by George Hudson

Setsuko Tsuchiya

I Love Liking You A Lot by Greg Hatala

Coming Soon
Lion's Way by Rita Ariyoshi
Hot Night in Budapest by Keith Rees
World Wakers by Briton E. Brookst

http://www.savantbooksandpublications.com
Enduring literary works for the twenty-first century

www.ingramcontent.com/pod-product-compliance
Lightning Source LLC
Chambersburg PA
CBHW070549160426
43199CB00014B/2425